History First

1066 - 1500

Acknowledgements

We are grateful to the following for permission to use photographs:

l = left, r = right, c = centre, t = top, b = bottom.

Bildarchiv Monheim GmbH/Alamy: p28 t; © Powered by Light/Alan Spencer/Alamy: p.110 t; Rolf Richardson/Alamy: p.63b; The Art Archive/Biblioteca Augusta Perugia/Dagli Orti: p.85;© Bibliothèque Royale Albert 1er, Belgium, ms 13076–77, fol 24 verso: p.100; Initial 'L' with Archbishop Lanfranc, from *Lanfranc, De Corpore et Sanguine Domini*, Normandy, c.1100. The Bodleian Library, University of Oxford, ms Bodl. 569, fol.1r: p.29t; Bibliothèque Inguimbertine, Carpetras, France/ The Bridgeman Art Library: p119b; Bibliothèque Municipale, Valenciennes, France/The Bridgeman Art Library: p118bl; Bibliothèque Nationale, Paris, France/The Bridgeman Art Library: p.103; The British Library, London, UK/The Bridgeman Art Library: pp.57b, 64t, 92, 97, 118br; © Chetham's Library, Manchester, UK/The Bridgeman Art Library: p.46; Department of the Environment, London, UK/The Bridgeman Art Library: p.62b; Eton College, Windsor, UK/The Bridgeman Art Library: p.104t; The Houses of Parliament, Westminster, London, UK/ The Bridgeman Art Library: pp.62–63t; Maison Jeanne d'Arc, Orleans, France/The Bridgeman Art Library: p.102; Musée de la Tapisserie, Bayeux, France. With special authorisation of the city of Bayeux/The Bridgeman Art Library: pp.9, 10–11, 12, 13, 16, 17, 18, 19; Private Collection/The Bridgeman Art Library: pp.86–87; Bristol Record Office: p.81; By permission of The British Library: pp.29b, 42, 56, 57t, 59, 98, 99, 118tl, 119br; Cadw, Crown Copyright: p.74; © The British Library/Heritage-Images: pp.64b, 82, 89; Icon/Ladd Co/Paramount/The Kobal Collection: p.76; Mary Evans Picture Library: pp.91, 119 tl & right; *Episode at the Coronation of William I*, © Museum of London: pp.6-7; Sandie Huskinson-Rolfe, PHOTOSEEKERS Picture Research: pp.34–35, 36–37; © David R. Ross: p.77; © Science Museum/Science & Society Picture Library: p.118tr; © Skyscan/E Clack: p.26; © Skyscan/E Nagele: p.28b; © 2004 Topfoto/Woodmansterne, The Bodleian Library, Oxford, UK: p.54; Topfoto/Uppa: p.83; 'The Battle of St Albans', reproduced by permission of the artist, Graham Turner – www.studio88. co.uk: p.104b; 'The Battle of Tewkesbury', reproduced by permission of the artist, Graham Turner: p110b; 'The Battle of Towton', reproduced by permission of the artist, Graham Turner: p111.

The quotation on pages 78–79 is taken from Matilda Bone by Karen Cushman (Random House 2002)

Original written sources have been simplified where necessary.

Pearson Education Limited
Edinburgh Gate
Harlow
Essex CM20 2JE
England

© Pearson Education Limited 2005

First published 2005

ISBN 0 582 85432 6

Designed by pentacor**big**, High Wycombe
Illustrated by Graham Kennedy and F&L Productions
Cover artwork by Reid Smith
Picture research by Sandie Huskinson-Rolfe of PHOTOSEEKERS

Contents

| 1066 | 1070 | 1080 | 1087 |

Jan 1066	20 Sept 1066	28 Sept 1066	14 Oct 1066	25 Dec 1066
Edward dies – Harold becomes king	Hardraada invades in the north	William lands in the south	The Battle of Hastings	William is crowned king

What do we know about William the Conqueror?

Interpreting the evidence

It was not a good beginning. Picture the scene. It was a winter's day in London. Perhaps it was frosty, foggy or windy. There might have been snow on the ground or it could have been raining. We don't know for certain. We do know it was Christmas Day and the year was 1066.

A crowd had gathered outside Westminster Abbey. It was waiting for William, **Duke** of Normandy. He was about to be crowned King of England. He arrived on horseback, dismounted and entered the abbey. He left Norman guards stationed outside because he still had many enemies among the **Saxon** population who did not accept his claim to the throne. Inside, he was greeted by Ealdred, the Archbishop of York. Ealdred conducted the ceremony. As it proceeded, there were cries of support from the Normans in the abbey. They were also heard by the guards outside. They interpreted them as the start of an English **rebellion** and an attack on the king. They began to set fire to the surrounding houses and attack the Saxons.

One Norman monk, writing 50 years later, had this to say:

SOURCE A

'As the fire spread rapidly, the people in the church were thrown into confusion. Crowds of them rushed outside, some to fight the fires, others to take the chance to go looting. Only the monks, the Archbishop and a few **clergy** remained … Though they were terrified, they managed to carry on and complete the coronation of the king, who was trembling violently.'

And so began the reign of William the Conqueror.

How do we know about William the Conqueror?
Let's use the evidence to find out.

NEW WORDS

Clergy
 people with religious duties
Duke
 very important ruler of a territory, nearly as powerful as a king
Rebellion
 attempt to get rid of a king or ruler
Saxons
 people who lived in England before the arrival of the Normans

ACTIVITIES

1. Look carefully at the painting in Source B. Can you find:
   a) Westminster Abbey
   b) King William
   c) Norman guards
   d) people rushing out of the abbey
   e) dead and injured Saxons
   f) burning buildings
   g) snow

2. The picture was painted early in the 20th Century. Do you think the painting shows exactly what happened in 1066? Explain your answer.

3. Now look back at Source A. Make a list of any similarities between this description and the picture.

4. Source A was written by a Norman monk 50 years after the coronation. Think about how its usefulness is affected by being written:
   a) by a Norman
   b) by a monk
   c) 50 years after the event it describes.

SOURCE B

The coronation of William I, early 20th Century

1066: The year of three kings

It was not certain that William should have been crowned king at all. He was not the only one with a claim to the English throne in 1066. His main rivals were Harold, **Earl** of Wessex and Harald Hardraada, King of Norway.

The problem was that the previous king, Edward the Confessor, had died on 5 January 1066 without any children. At that time the throne was usually inherited. In other words, the eldest surviving son was the heir and took over as king on the death of his father. But who should succeed Edward?

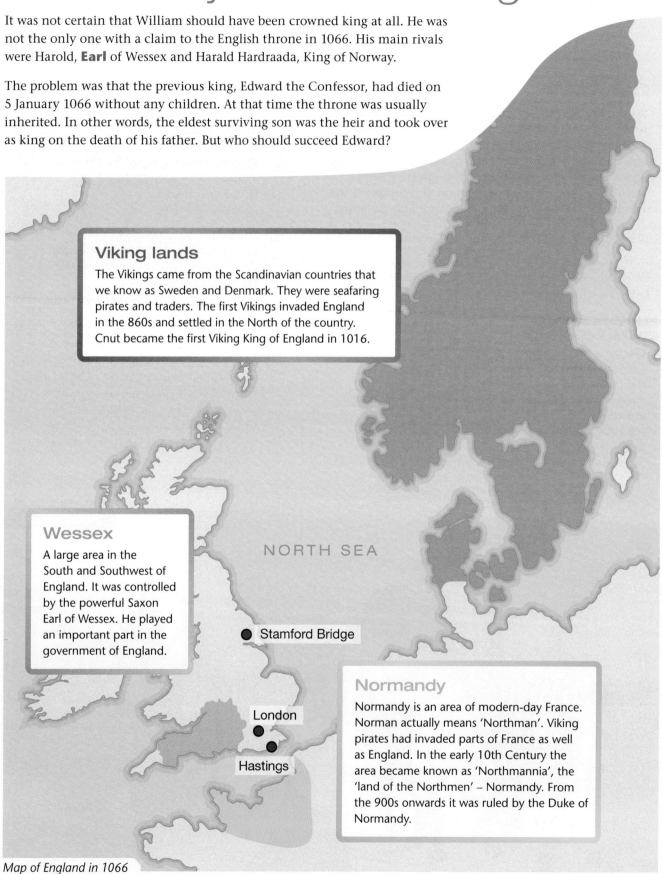

Viking lands

The Vikings came from the Scandinavian countries that we know as Sweden and Denmark. They were seafaring pirates and traders. The first Vikings invaded England in the 860s and settled in the North of the country. Cnut became the first Viking King of England in 1016.

Wessex

A large area in the South and Southwest of England. It was controlled by the powerful Saxon Earl of Wessex. He played an important part in the government of England.

NORTH SEA

● Stamford Bridge

Normandy

Normandy is an area of modern-day France. Norman actually means 'Northman'. Viking pirates had invaded parts of France as well as England. In the early 10th Century the area became known as 'Northmannia', the 'land of the Northmen' – Normandy. From the 900s onwards it was ruled by the Duke of Normandy.

London

Hastings

Map of England in 1066

The rival claims:
Who should be king?

Each of the contenders for the throne felt they had a very strong claim. Let's look at them in more detail.

William, Duke of Normandy

William, Duke of Normandy, was Edward's cousin. Edward's mother was a Norman. When the Viking, King Cnut, invaded England in 1016 and seized the throne, Edward had fled to Normandy. He stayed there until he became king in 1042. Afterwards he relied upon William's help to protect his throne from Viking attacks and from the powerful Earls of Wessex. It was William's soldiers who defeated the Earl of Wessex's rebellion against Edward in 1051.

Norman sources claim that Edward loved William like a son and was so pleased with him that, in 1051, he promised him the throne. They also say that in 1064, just two years before he died, Edward decided to make certain that William would be the next King of England. He sent Harold, Earl of Wessex to William in Normandy so that he could swear an **oath** that William would be the next king. He thought that, as a great English noble, Harold would have to support William if there was any trouble when he died.

Artist's impression of William, Duke of Normandy

NEW WORDS

Earl
  important and powerful landowner in England

Oath
  promise, often made in the name of God and considered very important at the time

SOURCE A

VBI HAROLD:SACRAMENTVM:FECIT: HIC HAROLD:DVX:
VVILLELMO DVCI:

Scene from the Bayeux Tapestry – The Oath

Harold, Earl of Wessex

Harold, Earl of Wessex, thought he should be the next king. He was Edward the Confessor's brother-in-law. He was also the only Englishman claiming the throne. Harold's family was the most powerful in England. They controlled Wessex and wanted to rule the whole country.

Harold became the most powerful nobleman in the country and the commander of Edward's army. In his old age, Edward left most of the business of governing England to Harold, who is said to have ruled well.

Scene from Bayeux Tapestry – Edward's deathbed scene, with Harold hovering over him

English sources say that although Harold had sworn an oath in 1064 agreeing that William would be the next king, this did not count. Harold had gone to Normandy to set free his nephew, who was being held there as a hostage. William is said to have told Harold that Edward had promised him, William, the throne. Harold could have his nephew only if he swore an oath on **holy relics** agreeing to William becoming king.

Saxon sources also claim that on his deathbed, Edward promised the throne to Harold as a reward for his loyalty and service. Saxon earls feared a Viking invasion, so a king was needed quickly. They accepted Harold's claim to the throne on 6 January 1066.

NEW WORDS

Holy relics
remains of an important holy person or object, thought to have great power

Artist's impression of Harold, Earl of Wessex

Harald Hardraada, King of Norway

The Viking, Harald Hardraada, King of Norway, felt he should be king. Many Vikings had settled in England and they had ruled England from 1016 to 1042. King Cnut (1016–40) was succeeded by his son, Harthacnut (1040–42). Harthacnut promised the throne to Harald Hardraada's father, but he died before Harthacnut. Harold, the Earl of Wessex's own brother, Tostig supported Hardraada's claim to the throne.

ACTIVITIES

1. Why do you think William, Harold, Earl of Wessex and Harald Hardraada all believed they had a strong claim to the throne?

2. Copy out and complete this sentence:

   'I think ... had the best claim to the throne of England in 1066 because ...'

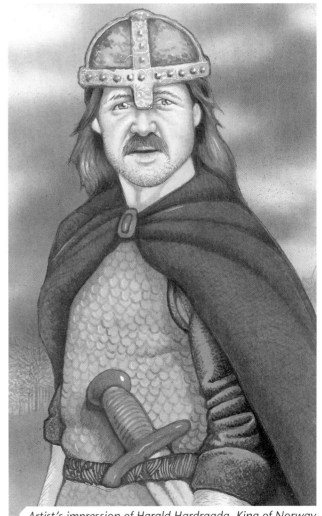

Artist's impression of Harald Hardraada, King of Norway

The story of 1066:
Why did William win?

Scene from Bayeux Tapestry – Harold receives bad news

It was not really surprising that Harold Godwinson, Earl of Wessex, became the next King of England. It did not mean that he had the best claim to the throne. It was quite simply that he was the most powerful Englishman, and he was in England.

When Edward the Confessor died on 5 January, the Saxon earls were already gathered together. Edward's greatest project, the building of Westminster Abbey, had just been completed and there was an official service of dedication on 28 December 1065, which Edward was too ill to attend. In the circumstances, the earls did not go home. Hurriedly, they were able to meet in their council, called a Witan, and accept Harold's claim to the throne. After all, if England did not have a king, it was more likely that rulers from Europe would invade.

Just 24 hours later, Westminster Abbey was the scene of Edward the Confessor's funeral. On the same day, and with great ceremony, Harold was crowned king there. Perhaps not quite what Edward had planned!

When the news of Harold's coronation reached William, out hunting in Normandy, he was furious. It was reported that he was so angry he could not speak! Harald Hardraada, King of Norway, was also very angry. They began to make their plans …

And so began the momentous year of 1066, a year that changed the course of English history.

William prepares

William began to prepare for an invasion of England. This was not easy. The problem was that Britain was an island. This meant that he had to get an army that was big enough to defeat Harold, and all its supplies, across the English Channel. Some of his advisers thought that it could not be done and would cost more than Normandy could afford. They told him not to go.

But William was determined. He believed he was the rightful King of England. Harold had sworn, on holy relics, to support his claim to the throne. Harold was an oath-breaker and that was a very serious thing. It meant that William got support from the Pope for his invasion of England and the Pope gave William a special banner.

William said his attack on England would be a 'holy **crusade**'. The appearance of a 'hairy star' or comet in the sky seemed to be an **omen**. People were very superstitious then and many believed it was a sign from God. It made William certain that God was angry with Harold and that he was right to prepare an invasion.

NEW WORDS

Crusade
   holy war, blessed by the Pope.

Omen
   event that suggests something good or bad is going to happen

So, trees were chopped down and boats were built. William already had a well-trained army of knights, archers and foot soldiers. He increased it to 5,000 foot soldiers and 2,000 knights by getting help from other parts of France, such as Brittany and Flanders. England was a rich country, so he promised to reward them with English land when he won. By the summer everything was ready, but he could not set sail … the wind was blowing in the wrong direction.

Scene from Bayeux Tapestry – chopping down trees to build boats

Finding out about William

At the end of this unit you are going to write an obituary for William. An obituary is written just after someone has died. It looks back over their life and tells you what sort of a person they were and what they did.

From the story so far you will find evidence to show that William was:

a) determined
b) organised
c) religious.

Make a copy of this table. If you have access to a computer you could use a word processing program such as Word to create a table. Complete the entries for 'organised' and 'religious' from what you have read already. You will be adding to this table later, so make each box large enough for more detail to be added.

What we know about William	Evidence	Source of information
Determined	He was determined to win the English throne from Harold.	Bayeux Tapestry
Organised		
Religious		

The diversion in the North

Harold knew that the Normans were preparing to invade and he prepared to stop them. He gathered together the largest army ever seen in England. All summer, both his army and his fleet waited on the south coast – until early September. By that time his army was running out of food and many of his soldiers had to go home to harvest their crops. Soon after this gales destroyed many of his ships in the Channel.

Then, on 20 September, Harald Hardraada invaded the North of England. He was supported by Harold's own brother, Tostig. About 300 ships are said to have arrived off the coast of Yorkshire, carrying Viking warriors. The local English earls, Edwin and Morcar, led an army against the Vikings, but were defeated in a battle at Fulford, near York. Hardraada went to York to eat, drink and relax. He knew Harold was miles away. He didn't expect what happened next …

Harold quickly gathered his army together and marched over 300 kilometres north at great speed. On 25 September, the English king launched a surprise attack on Hardraada at Stamford Bridge. A fierce and bloody battle raged, but the Viking force was defeated. Both Hardraada and Tostig were dead, along with hundreds of their men. Only 24 ships were needed to take what was left of the army home. It was a great victory, but …

There was no time to celebrate. Just two days later, on 27 September, the wind in the Channel changed direction. William could finally set sail with his invasion fleet. It landed in Pevensey on the south coast on 28 September. And Harold was stuck in the North!

The Normans were able to gather food, build a secure camp and relax without fear. King Harold now had to rush his exhausted soldiers over 400 kilometres back south. Many of his foot soldiers got left behind. They simply couldn't keep up. Harold paused in London, but then rushed on to meet William. On the night of 13 October he arrived at Hastings, knowing that there would be battle the next day.

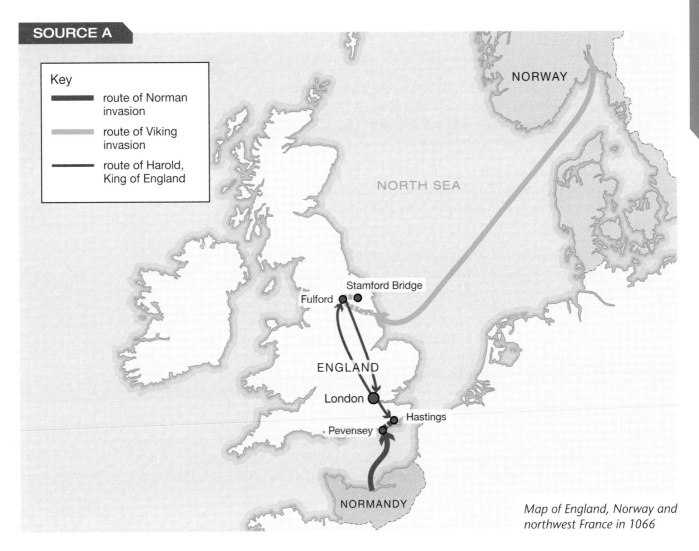

Key

— route of Norman invasion

— route of Viking invasion

— route of Harold, King of England

NORWAY

NORTH SEA

Stamford Bridge

Fulford

ENGLAND

London

Hastings

Pevensey

NORMANDY

Map of England, Norway and northwest France in 1066

ACTIVITY

Using the information from the diversion in the North, write a timetable of key events. You might want to start like this:

Date	Event
Summer 1066	Harold's army and fleet wait for William's invasion on the south coast of England ...
20 September 1066	

Finding out about William

1. Add any new information you think is important in columns 2 and 3 of the table you started on page 14.

2. Add 'Lucky' to Column 1 of your table and complete the other columns.

The battle

Early on the morning of 14 October, Harold placed his army on top of Senlac Hill and waited for William. His best men were at the front. These were the **housecarls**, armed with double-handed axes, which could cut through a man and horse with a single blow. Harold's soldiers used their shields to form a tight 'wall'.

When the battle started, the fighting was fierce. The Norman knights, armed with spears, kept charging up the hill. The Norman archers fired their arrows, but they could not break through the Saxon shield wall, until …

Some Normans, hearing a rumour that William had been killed, turned and began to flee. But William was still very much alive. He pulled off his helmet for all to see and rallied his soldiers to renew the attack.

Some of the English had chased after the fleeing Normans. This broke up the shield wall. So the Normans used the tactic again … and again. Each time the English broke ranks to pursue the retreating Normans. The Norman knights turned and slaughtered them, time and time again. By evening, Harold had very few men left at the top of the hill and still the Norman knights attacked and the archers fired their arrows.

Finally, Harold was killed. With nothing left to fight for, some of the remaining English soldiers fled. After nine hours of fighting, in which thousands of men had been killed and injured, the battle was finally over and William had won.

We know about the events of 1066 from the evidence that has survived. One of the most useful sources is the Bayeux Tapestry. It is very long (about 70 metres and long enough to go around your classroom) and quite narrow (about 48 centimetres). It was made in England, probably on the orders of Bishop Odo of Bayeux, William's half brother, soon after 1066. It tells the Norman story of the invasion in a series of pictures, rather like a strip cartoon. You have already seen some of the scenes from the Tapestry on pages 9 to 13. There are several more on the next two pages.

NEW WORDS

Housecarls
member of very best Saxon troops, usually used as a bodyguard by Harold and the earls

SOURCE A

...NT:HAROLDO: hIC RE SIDET:HAROLD
...NA   REGIS   REX:AN   GLORVM:
                                STIGANT
                                ARCHI:EPS

...ODO:EPS:BA.CVLV.IENENS.   C.N.OR.   hIC EST   DVX
                                              VVILLE...
                                 TAT.
                                 PVE.
                                 ROS.

...M: hIC PORTA TVR:CORPVS:EADWARDI:REGIS:AD:ECCLESIAM:SCI.
                                            PETRI   APLI

SOURCE G

SOURCE H

EXEVNT:CABALLI   DE NAVIBVS ·- ET hIC:MI LITES:

ACTIVITIES

Have you noticed that these scenes are not in the correct order? They have been mixed up.

1. Read back over the story of 1066 on pages 12–16 and see if you can put the scenes on pages 16 to 19 in the correct order.

2. For each scene, write a sentence or two describing what is happening. The first one has been started for you.

   Source D: Edward the Confessor is buried in Westminster Abbey.

Finding out about William

Now add 'Brave soldier' and 'Cunning' to column 1 of the table you began on page 14.
Using the information and evidence in the last section, complete columns 2 and 3.

How did William conquer England?

The Battle of Hastings was won. Harold was dead. But William still had to take control of England. He had conquered one small corner of the country. He faced a hostile population of between one and two million people. He had just 10,000 men to help him. It seemed an impossible task. Yet William not only gained control, he also stayed in control for over 20 years. So, how did he conquer England?

Gaining control

Becoming king

To become king, William had to take control of London, England's capital city. But some of Harold's troops, who had got left behind on the march to Hastings, were still in London and could cause problems.

William was also unsure how the powerful northern earls, Edwin and Morcar, would react. They had not fought at Hastings. Would they try to stop him becoming king? What about the people of London? How would they react?

What should William do? He had two main options. He could:

a) march straight to London, risking a battle with the remaining Saxon soldiers

b) go very slowly, giving the Saxons time to decide what to do.

....

What would you have done?

SOURCE A

'Then William marched to Dover, which was held by a large force. The English were stricken with fear and prepared to surrender, but our men, greedy for booty, set fire to the castle and the greater part of it was destroyed. The Duke, unwilling that those who had offered to surrender should suffer loss, gave them money for the damage. Having taken possession of the castle, the Duke spent eight days adding new fortifications to it.'

Written by William of Poitiers around 1071
[He fought for William the Conqueror]

SOURCE B

'William was **laying waste** Sussex, Kent, Hampshire, Surrey, Middlesex and Hertfordshire. He burned villages and slaughtered the inhabitants. He was then met by the earls Edwin and Morcar and Londoners of the better sort, who submitted to him.

Written by Florence of Worcester, a Saxon monk. He is describing William's movements before he went to London

ACTIVITIES

Look at Sources A–C carefully.

1. What did William choose to do?

2. Why do you think William secured the castle in Dover first? (Clue: look at the map)

3. Why do you think his army burned and destroyed the countryside as it approached London?

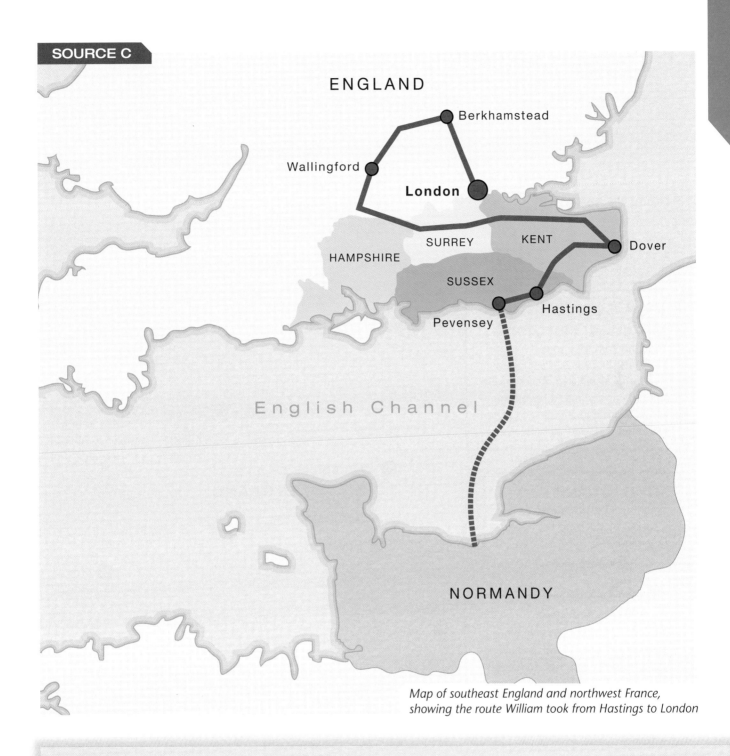

ENGLAND

Berkhamstead

Wallingford

London

SURREY

HAMPSHIRE

KENT

Dover

SUSSEX

Hastings

Pevensey

English Channel

NORMANDY

*Map of southeast England and northwest France,
showing the route William took from Hastings to London*

Finding out about William

1. Using the section on how William became king, add more details to column 2 of your table to support the points you already have in column 1. Don't forget to note the source of your information.

2. There is evidence in this section that William was ruthless. Add 'Ruthless' to column 1 and then complete columns 2 and 3.

3. Add any other points about William that you think are important to your table.

Crushing rebellions

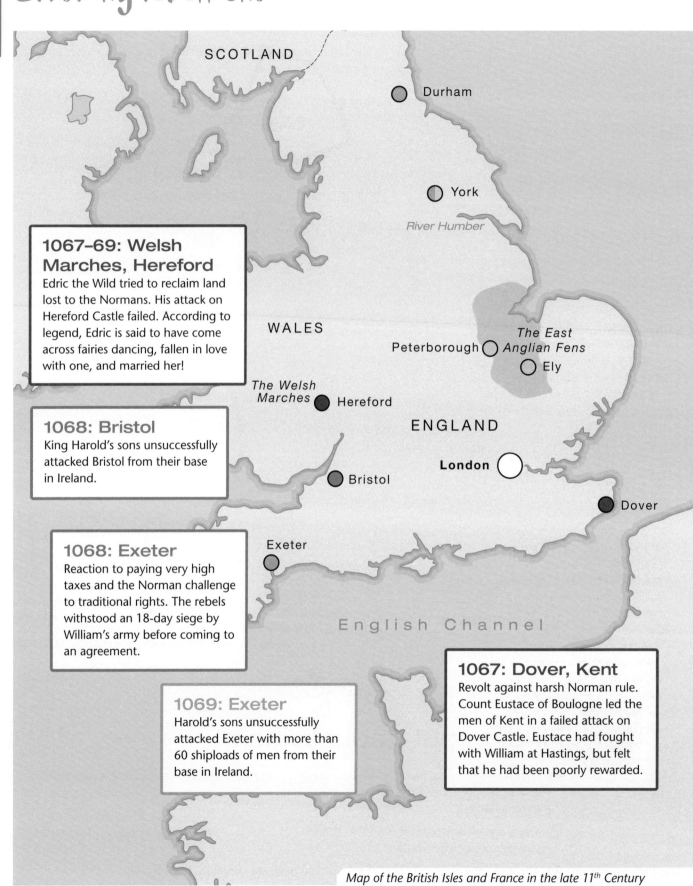

SCOTLAND

● Durham

◐ York

River Humber

1067–69: Welsh Marches, Hereford

Edric the Wild tried to reclaim land lost to the Normans. His attack on Hereford Castle failed. According to legend, Edric is said to have come across fairies dancing, fallen in love with one, and married her!

WALES

Peterborough ◐ *The East Anglian Fens*

◯ Ely

The Welsh Marches ● Hereford

1068: Bristol

King Harold's sons unsuccessfully attacked Bristol from their base in Ireland.

ENGLAND

London ◯

● Bristol

● Dover

1068: Exeter

Reaction to paying very high taxes and the Norman challenge to traditional rights. The rebels withstood an 18-day siege by William's army before coming to an agreement.

Exeter ◐

English Channel

1067: Dover, Kent

Revolt against harsh Norman rule. Count Eustace of Boulogne led the men of Kent in a failed attack on Dover Castle. Eustace had fought with William at Hastings, but felt that he had been poorly rewarded.

1069: Exeter

Harold's sons unsuccessfully attacked Exeter with more than 60 shiploads of men from their base in Ireland.

Map of the British Isles and France in the late 11th Century

1069: York, Durham, River Humber

The northern earls, Edwin and Morcar, who had previously promised their loyalty to William, rebelled when faced with paying higher taxes. They were supported by King Malcolm of Scotland and King Sven of Denmark. Both these kings wanted to gain land and wealth for their country. Hundreds of Normans were killed at York.

1075: York

Earl Waltheof, the last powerful English earl, made an **alliance** with two French lords against William. With Danish help they **looted** York, but they did not attempt to overthrow William.

1070–71: Ely, the Fens, Peterborough

The King of Denmark brought reinforcements across the North Sea and attacked the Fens of East Anglia – a wide area of flat, marshy land full of swamps and streams. Peterborough was **sacked** and the Isle of Ely was occupied as a base. The Danes were joined by Earls Edwin and Morcar, as well as other English rebels. The most famous of these was Hereward the Wake, so-called because he was always wide-awake and watchful. It was said that Hereward could kill a man with his fists, that he could fight 12 men at once with his sword, Brainbiter, and that his horse, Swallow, was faster than any other.

Even after his coronation, William's control was not complete. The English did not give up without a fight. Between 1067 and 1075 William spent most of the time when he was in England putting down rebellions against his rule. Some rebellions were very small, but others were very serious.

There were a number of different reasons why rebellions occurred. Here are some of them:

- rivals for the throne attacked William
- Saxons reacted to harsh Norman rule
- attempts to recover land taken by the Normans
- an opportunity to rape and **pillage**
- towns felt their rights were threatened
- Saxons disliked paying high taxes (called 'geld')
- Saxon resistance to Norman rule
- an opportunity to gain more land.

ACTIVITIES

1. Using both the list of reasons why rebellions occurred and the information on the map, complete your own copy of this table. Remember, there might be more than one reason for some of the rebellions.

Date of rebellion (chronological order)	Part of country	Reason(s) for rebellion
1067		
1067–69		
1068		
1068		
1069		
1069		
1070–71		
1075		

2. Which rebellion do you think was the most dangerous to William? Why?

NEW WORDS

Alliance
   agreement to work together
Looted
   stole goods from an enemy
Pillage
   steal
Sacked
   robbed and destroyed

How did William deal with the rebels?

All the rebellions against the Normans failed. There were several reasons for this. As you have seen, the rebellions had different causes and were not co-ordinated. Also, most English people did not rebel, and there was no strong alternative to William as king. Even the Danes didn't want to rule England. They simply wanted to take as much loot as possible. But the rebellions also failed because of the way William dealt with them.

Read the Sources A–D carefully. They describe how William dealt with some of the more important rebellions.

SOURCE A

'At last, the chief citizens were forced to ask for mercy. A procession went out to the King and knelt at his feet. The King pardoned them. The people of Exeter were full of joy. William did not take their goods away. He posted trusted soldiers at the city gates, to stop the army coming in and looting. He then marched into Cornwall, quickly restored order, disbanded his army, and was home in time for Easter.'

Odericus Vitalis, a monk in Normandy, wrote his history about 1125. His father was Norman and his mother was English

SOURCE B

'The royal forces approached York, only to learn that the Danes had fled. The king ordered his men to hunt out the enemy. He cut down many in his anger; and burned homes to ashes. Nowhere else had William shown such cruelty. He punished the innocent with the guilty. In his anger he ordered that all crops, herds and food of every kind should be burned to ashes, so that the whole region could not feed the people. As a result there was such a terrible famine that more than 100,000 young and old alike perished of hunger.'

Also written by Odericus Vitalis

ACTIVITIES

1. Read Source A. How did William deal with the rebels in Exeter?

2. Read Source B. How did William deal with the rebellion in York?

3. Why do you think William acted so differently in York?

4. Read Source C. How did William manage to defeat Hereward the Wake? Why did the monks of Ely help him?

5. Read Source D. Who helped William defeat Waltheof? What does that tell you about William's control of the country by 1075?

6. Did the way William deal with rebellions change from 1067–75? How? Why might this be so?

NEW WORDS

Disbanded
sent home

Enchantment
using 'magic' to win

Vengeance
the worst punishment

Finding out about William

Have you learnt anything new about William? Is there anything you could add to column 1 of your table? (Clue: look at Source D and your answer to Activity 1.)

Keeping control

From the moment William and his army landed in England in 1066, they had to defend themselves. It took William several years to put down all the rebellions against him. At the same time he was taking steps to secure his conquest and keep control.

Building castles

During William's 20-year reign, over 80 **motte and bailey** castles were built all over England. In the courtyard there would be living quarters, kitchens, stables, storage huts and workshops.

The castles were built in case of immediate danger or to control important towns, ports, rivers or roads. Where possible they were built on a hill or cliff to make them more difficult to attack.

The first one was built at Hastings in the two weeks between William's landing at Pevensey and the Battle of Hastings.

SOURCE A

Aerial photograph of Mountfitchet Castle, showing all key features

'The nobles order the peasants to make a mound of earth as high as they can and round it they dig a ditch as wide and deep as possible. On the top of the mound they make a fort of very strong logs firmly fixed together. Within the fort is a house, a central keep which overlooks the rest of the castle. The entrance to the fortress is across a bridge over the ditch and through an entrance gate.'

Written by Walter the Archdeacon, a French priest, in about 1100

'Buildings were knocked down or abandoned to make way for the construction of a timber castle and its defences. Domesday Book refers to 98 houses being enclosed by the castle ... The first castle was established in 1067 or 1068. The site selected was a natural ridge overlooking a river valley. Twelve large fragments of a gatehouse were found, having later collapsed into the **barbican** ditch. Lying within a small courtyard at the foot of the motte bridge was a well ...'

From Recent Excavations at Norwich Castle *by Elizabeth Shepherd Popescu, 1997*

ACTIVITIES

1. Look carefully at Source A and find:
   a) the 'motte'
   b) the ditch or 'moat'
   c) the fort or 'stockade'
   d) the house or 'keep'
   e) the bridge
   f) the entrance gate
   g) the 'bailey'
   h) the houses or living quarters
   i) the kitchens
   j) the stables
   k) the storage huts
   l) the workshops
   m) the well

2. Why do you think the Normans were so keen to build motte and bailey castles?

3. Can you think of any disadvantages or weaknesses of motte and bailey castles? (Clue: what were they made of?)

NEW WORDS

Barbican
   fortified gateway on the way into a castle
Motte and bailey
   mound (motte) that a castle was built on; courtyard (bailey) around the castle

Finding out about William

Think about what you have learnt in this section about William as a king and a leader. You should now be able to add lots more detail to columns 2 and 3 of your table.

Strengthening the Church

William's invasion of England in 1066 was supported by the Pope. The Pope gave William a special banner and William said his attack on England would be a holy crusade.

While William was king, many new cathedrals, churches, abbeys and monasteries were built across the country. They were much larger than the Saxon churches they replaced and very different in style. The whole country seemed to have turned into a gigantic building site.

As well as building new churches, William also appointed new leaders. Nearly all the existing Church leaders were replaced by Normans loyal to William.

SOURCE B *Inside Lincoln Cathedral*

SOURCE A

The building of Lincoln Cathedral begun while William was king

Archbishop Lanfranc

SOURCE D

Lanfranc was born in Italy in about 1010. He became a monk in Normandy in 1042 and Abbot of Caen in 1063. He had an international reputation as a brilliant scholar. William made him Archbishop of Canterbury in 1070 to reform and reorganise the Church in England. When the king was in Normandy, Lanfranc played a leading role in running the country. He died in 1089.

William gave lots of land to the new cathedrals and monasteries. This made them rich and powerful. Their support helped William keep control of the country. The clergy were often the only people who could read and write, so many also helped William to run the country.

At this time religion played a very important part in peoples' lives. They went to church on Sundays and holy days. They listened to the clergy telling them how to live good lives by following the teachings of the Bible, so that they would go to heaven and not hell.

SOURCE E

'Their coming to England revived the rule of religion which had … grown lifeless. You might see churches rise in every village, or in the towns and cities, monasteries built after a style unknown before: you could watch the country flourishing with renewed religious observance.'

Written by William of Malmesbury

SOURCE F

William holding the Church in his hand

ACTIVITIES

1. Which of these statements best describes how William dealt with the Church?
   a) William wanted to destroy the Church.
   b) William wanted to make the Church stronger.
   c) William wanted to control the Church.

2. Write a paragraph to explain your choice of statement.

Finding out about William

Think about what you have learnt about William in this section. You should be able to add lots more detail to columns 2 and 3 in your table.

Sharing the land

William used land to help him control England. He gave land to those who supported him. Land meant power and wealth. Many Saxon earls had died in the battles of 1066. Others had fled abroad. William gave their land to the Normans who had helped him conquer England. In return they had duties to perform. This system of rewards and duties was called the feudal system.

ACTIVITIES

1. The diagram below represents the feudal system.
   Use the information in the text to complete the empty boxes.

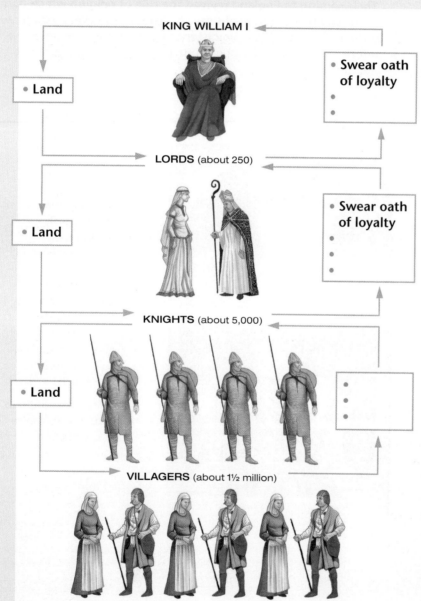

KING WILLIAM I

- Land

- Swear oath of loyalty
-
-

LORDS (about 250)

- Land

- Swear oath of loyalty
-
-

KNIGHTS (about 5,000)

- Land

-
-
-

VILLAGERS (about 1½ million)

Lords

The king owned all the land in England. He kept some for himself, most of it for hunting. He used the rest to reward his barons and bishops, the lords. In return for their land, the barons and bishops had to swear an oath of loyalty to the king. They also had to help the king keep law and order in their area, and they had to provide him with soldiers.

Knights

The lords kept some of the land for their own use. They gave the rest to their supporters, the knights. Each of them became the lord of a manor. In return, the knights had to swear an oath of loyalty to their lord. They also had to help keep law and order in their area, and they had to provide the lord with military service. This might involve fighting, escorting the lord on journeys or guarding the lord's castle for a certain number of days a year.

Villagers

The knights kept some of the land for their own use. They gave the rest to their villagers. In return, the villagers had to swear an oath of loyalty to the knight. They also had to pay taxes and work on the knight's land for a certain number of days a year.

2. Use your completed diagram to explain to your neighbour how the feudal system helped William keep control of the country.

Surveying the land

At Christmas in 1085 William ordered a survey of all the land in England. Royal officials were sent all round the country to find out about every village. Their findings were collected together and recorded by monks in the Domesday Book. It was a huge task, but it was completed in just one year.

Historians are not sure why William ordered the Domesday survey. He may have wanted better information for raising taxes. So much land had changed hands since 1066 that no one knew exactly who held what. And in 1085 he was certainly concerned that the King of Denmark was planning an invasion. William would need to know how much he could tax people. The invasion didn't happen, but William brought a huge army over from Normandy and it had to be paid for.

SOURCE A

Better-off farmers

1 hide was the amount of land needed to support one family.

Domesday name

Ploughs were used to prepare the land for planting crops. Each plough was pulled by eight oxen. The number of ploughs usually showed how wealthy a village was.

> ELSTOW (ELNESTOV) answers for 3½ hides. The nuns of St. Mary's hold it from Countess Judith. Land for seven ploughs. In lordship 2 ploughs. 14 villagers have 5 plough. 11 smallholders and 4 slaves. 1 mill at 24s; meadow for 4 ploughs; woodland, 60 pigs. Value 100s; when aquired 40s; before 1066 £10. 4 Freeman held this manor. They were King Edward's men.

Farmed by the nuns themselves

Landless villagers

£5

Annual rent paid to the manor

provided fuel, building material and autumn grazing for animals.

£2

Common land for hay, needed for feeding oxen in winter

Small farmers who rented their land from the local lord

Poor villagers who worked for the lord and also looked after a small plot in their own time to feed their families.

ACTIVITIES

1. The Domesday Book collected information that William felt was important at the time. If you were to make a Domesday Book today, what sort of information would you want to record in it? Make a list of some of the questions you would ask.

2. From the information on Elstow in the Domesday Book, what questions do you think William asked?

3. Is Elstow richer in 1086 than in 1066, or poorer?

4. Does the Domesday Book show that William had very strong or very weak control of England?

5. 'Domesday' means Day of Judgement. Who do you think gave it this name and why?

6. Why is the Domesday Book such an important piece of evidence for historians?

Finding out about William

Think about what you have learnt about William on pages 30 and 31. You should be able to add lots more detail to columns 2 and 3 of your table.

Remembering William

William died in 1087. He had been fighting the King of France to prevent him from taking some of his lands. His horse threw him violently against the front of his saddle. He was seriously injured. A few days later he died. A magnificent funeral was planned.

William had grown quite fat as he got older. The coffin was too small. As his body was forced in, it burst. The smell was dreadful. Only the monks taking the funeral service stayed, holding their noses. It was an unexpected and gruesome end to a remarkable life.

An artist's representation of King William's funeral

So, how should we remember William? This is what two monks, writing in the *Anglo-Saxon Chronicle*, had to say soon after his death:

SOURCE A

'This king raised castles and crushed the poor
He took gold and silver and so much more.
There was no fairness in his deeds
He simply fed his deepest greed.
He loved to hunt for stags and boars
He took our land and made this law:
The eyes of poachers who steal from their lord
Must be cut out with the point of a sword.'

Anglo-Saxon chronicle

ACTIVITIES

1 In what ways do Sources A and B agree?

2 In what ways do these sources disagree?

SOURCE B

'King William was stronger than any king before. He was so gentle to the good men and stern to those who disobeyed him. Also he was very violent, so that no one dared to do anything against his will. The good peace he made in this country is not to be forgotten.

An honest man could travel over his kingdom without injury with his pockets full of gold. William protected deer and boar and loved the stags so much as if he were their father. These things we have written about him, both good and bad, that good men may copy the good points and avoid the bad.'

Anglo-Saxon chronicle

Finding out about William

1 Add anything else you think is important from this section to your table.

2 Can you find any contradictions in the information in your table? What are they?

3 Why do you think there are contradictions? (Clue: look at the source of your information.)

Writing your obituary of William

You should now be ready to write your obituary of William. The following points should help.

Selecting information

- Which things are you going to include as 'big ideas' in William's life and which will you leave out?

- Which 'little ideas' can you use to support your big ideas?

- Select your information carefully. You do not have to use all the information in your table and you don't have to use it in the same order either.

Interpreting William

- What do you now think of William the Conqueror?

- Remember, Norman sources from the time will tend to support William, whereas Saxon sources would probably be quite critical.

Reconstructing history

Sources are used to help us recreate a picture of the past. Take a look at the pictures on pages 34–37. They were all taken at Mountfitchet Castle (see page 26) in Essex where the past has been 'reconstructed'. What do they tell us about Norman times?

How do historians really know what life was like in Norman times? Have you ever wondered how historians find out about the past?

Historians use evidence that has survived from the time. There might be some written records or perhaps some visual sources. Sometimes there are physical remains to examine or **archaeological evidence** to use.

SOURCE A

The reconstruction of a room in a rich Norman house at Mountfitchet Castle.

ACTIVITIES

Look at Source A carefully. It is supposed to be the inside of a rich Norman house. What items would you expect to see in a rich house today?

Write a list of as many things, such as washing machines, that you would expect to see today. Try to imagine what it must have been like to live without these things.

NEW WORDS

Archaeological evidence
actual remains from historical periods found in the ground

Living conditions

SOURCE B

Part of the bailey

SOURCE C

A house

SOURCE D

A well

 **ACTIVITIES**

Using Sources B–D and the aerial photos on page 26, think about the following:

- space in the bailey
- how many people might have lived there
- what building materials were used for the doors, walls, windows and roof?
- which materials were available in Norman times
- which materials weren't available in Norman times
- how buildings were heated
- how they were lit
- how clothes were washed
- how buildings were cleaned
- what happened to rubbish
- what was rubbish then
- how food was cooked.

Food and drink

SOURCE E

An ox

SOURCE F

Chicken runs

SOURCE G

Pig sty

👁 **ACTIVITIES**

Using Sources E–G, think about the following:

- what people might have eaten
- what other food would have been available at the time
- what people certainly wouldn't have eaten.

Working **conditions**

SOURCE H

The candle maker

SOURCE I

The blacksmith

SOURCE J

The herbalist

ACTIVITIES

1. Using Sources H–J, think about the following:
   - why were these jobs important in a Norman motte and bailey castle
   - what other workshops there might have been

2. What do all the photographs tell us about life in Norman times?
   a) Look back at all the evidence about life in Norman England in this unit. Does it agree with what you can see of Mountfitchet Castle?
   b) Do you think the people at Mountfitchet Castle have got their reconstruction right? What changes would you make to the displays?

Medieval monarchs

WILLIAM I (reigned **1066–1087**)

Robert
(Duke of Normandy)

WILLIAM II
(reigned 1087–00)

HENRY I *m* **Matilda**
(reigned 1100–35)

William
(Drowned 1120)

William II

William II never married and had no children. He was known as William Rufus. Rufus means red and William, who had a terrible temper was often red-faced! When he was king he made the people of England pay very high taxes. He spent a lot of his reign trying to conquer Normandy and fighting his elder brother, Robert.

William Rufus built Westminster Hall and the first stone bridge across the River Thames in London.

He was killed by an arrow when out hunting in the New Forest.

Henry I

Henry was the youngest son of William the Conqueror. People whispered that he had been involved in the death of his brother. When William II died, Henry rushed to Winchester and seized the **treasury**. He then went to Westminster Abbey and was crowned king three days later.

In 1106, Henry beat his elder brother Robert in battle and locked him up for the rest of his life. Henry was known as strong and ruthless.

Henry was the first Norman king who could read or write. He founded England's first zoo in the Tower of London.

His heir was drowned whilst sailing off the coast of Normandy.

What did people expect of a medieval monarch?

- **Family Man.** He was expected to produce a son to succeed him.
- **Policeman.** People should be able to go about their business in safety.
- **Judge.** Trials should be fair for everyone.
- **Defender of the Empire.** He was expected to lead his army in battle, and win.
- **Protector of the Church.** The Church was rich and powerful, led by the Pope in Rome. The king was expected to respect the views of the Church.

NEW WORDS

Civil war
A war between different groups in the same country.

Legitimate
A child whose parents were married

Treasury
Place where the governments money was kept

1110	1120	1130	1140	1150	1154

1087–1100	1100–1135	1120	1135–1154	1138–1141	1141–1147	1154
William II, known as Rufus	Henry I	Death of William, son of Henry I	Stephen	Matilda leads rebellion against Stephen	Matilda imprisoned by Stephen	Henry II

Adela *m* Stephen of Blois

MATILDA *m* Geoffrey of Anjou
(reigned Apr–Nov 1141)

STEPHEN *m* Matilda of Boulogne
(reigned 1135–54)

HENRY II *m* Eleanor of Aquitane
(reigned 1154–89)

Eustace
(died 1153)

Matilda

Matilda was the only surviving **legitimate** child of Henry I. When her father was alive the barons agreed she would be the next ruler. But she was a woman and her husband was an enemy of the Normans. From 1138, Matilda came over to England and led a rebellion against Stephen, Henry's nephew. In 1141 she defeated him at Lincoln and imprisoned him. But the barons still would not accept her as queen and she was never crowned.

Stephen's men beat her later that year in Oxford.

In 1147 Matilda went back to Anjou and left the fighting to her son, Henry.

Stephen

Stephen was Henry's favourite nephew. When Henry I died, Stephen rushed over from France and claimed the throne of England. For most of his reign he was involved in a **civil war** with Matilda. He was never firmly in control of the country. Many barons took this as an opportunity to extend their own powers and build castles.

In many ways Stephen was the most attractive of the Norman kings. He was charming, good natured and friendly. Before he died in 1154, he named Matilda's son Henry II as his heir.

ACTIVITIES

1 What relation was Matilda to William the Conqueror?

2 What relation was Stephen to Matilda?

3 Who would you have expected to be William the Conqueror's heir?

4 Why didn't Matilda become Queen in 1135?

5 What does this tell you about Norman attitudes to women?

6 Think about how each Norman king became ruler. What does this tell us about how the succession was decided? Are there any common factors?

7 Do you think:
a) William II
b) Henry I
c) Stephen
d) Matilda
were successful rulers? Use the list 'What did people expect of a medieval king?' to help you decide.

EXTENSION ACTIVITY

You might like to find out more about these monarchs. They all have plenty of skeletons in their cupboards! You could use library books, CD-ROMs or the Internet to help you produce a more detailed biography of one of them.

The life of a monk

'Hello! My name is Brother Thomas. You'll see a lot of me in the next unit. I'm a Benedictine monk in Ely Abbey. The monks here helped King William to put down Hereward's rebellion in 1071. That was a bit before my time, though!'

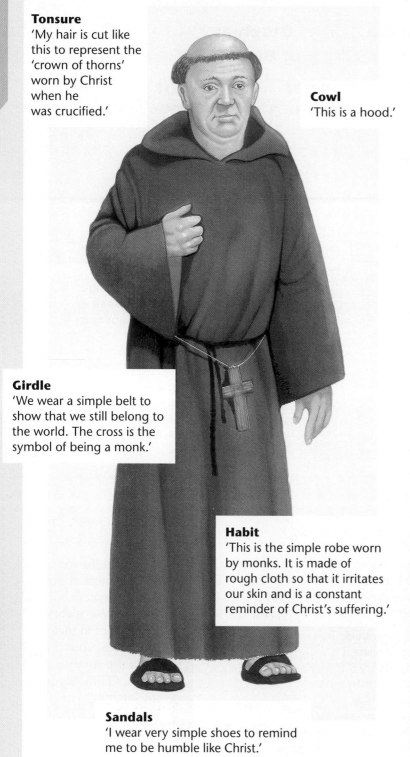

Tonsure
'My hair is cut like this to represent the 'crown of thorns' worn by Christ when he was crucified.'

Cowl
'This is a hood.'

Girdle
'We wear a simple belt to show that we still belong to the world. The cross is the symbol of being a monk.'

Habit
'This is the simple robe worn by monks. It is made of rough cloth so that it irritates our skin and is a constant reminder of Christ's suffering.'

Sandals
'I wear very simple shoes to remind me to be humble like Christ.'

'I came to the abbey in 1167. I've lived here for 23 years now. My family were quite rich, but I chose to give my life to the service of God. So, I gave up all my possessions and came to live here, where I'm cut off from the world. I'm not allowed to marry, I eat only the simplest food, my clothes are very plain and quite rough to wear and I sleep in a bare room. I spend my time praying and working inside the abbey. I'm the scribe here, so I keep all the written records, or chronicles. It usually is monks who produce books as most people can't read or write. Other monks have different jobs, such as caring for the sick or working on the land to produce our food.'

'I'm very content with my life here. We believe that if we lead good Christian lives, we will gain our reward in heaven. The idea of going to hell and being punished forever is just awful. We also pray for other people outside the abbey. Rich people often give us money to do this. They think it will help them get to heaven. Sometimes we are even given land. Some abbeys and monasteries have become very rich as a result.'

'As Ely is a Benedictine abbey, we follow the rules of St Benedict. There are other religious orders such as the Cistercians, Carthusians and Augustinians. They have different rules, as well as habits. Have a look at some of our most important rules and the timetable for our day.'

Benedictine monastery rules

- No one should do just what he wants or argue with the abbot.
- All monks should take turns to wait on each other.
- No one should be excused kitchen work.
- At mealtimes there should always be a Bible reading.
- There should be complete silence at table and no whispering.
- The brothers should pass food to each other. If anything should be wanted, signs should be used.
- Above all, care should be taken of the sick.
- In the Bible it says 'Seven times in the day do I praise thee', so there should be seven church services a day.
- Laziness leads to sin. The brothers should be busy with manual work when they are not reading or praying.
- A mattress, woollen blanket and pillow should be enough bedding.

A monk's timetable

Time	Activity
1.45 am	wake up, then private reading and prayer
2.00 am	church service
3.30 am	sleep (summer only)
4.00 am	church service
5.00 am	private reading and prayer
6.00 am	church service, then eat
7.00 am	work
8.00 am	church service
9.15 am	work
11.45 am	church service
midday	**meal**
1.00 pm	private reading and prayer
1.45 pm	sleep (summer only)
2.45 pm	church service
3.00 pm	work
5.45 pm	meal
6.00 pm	church service
7.15 pm	private reading and prayer
7.45 pm	church service
8.00 pm	bed

ACTIVITIES

1 Make a list of all the ways in which you think the life of a monk was easy.

2 Make a list of all the ways in which you think the life of a monk was hard.

3 Why did the Church become so rich?

NEW WORDS

Abbot
head of an abbey or monastery

EXTENSION ACTIVITY
Choose one of the other religious orders mentioned in this section. Try to find out how it was different from the Benedictine order.

1133

Henry was born

1149

Henry lands in England to fight against Stephen

1152

Henry marries Eleanor of Aquitaine

1153

Henry invades England and is accepted as heir to Stephen

1154

Henry becomes King of England

1155

Henry pulls down over 300 illegal castles

Becket is made Chancellor

How successful was Henry II?

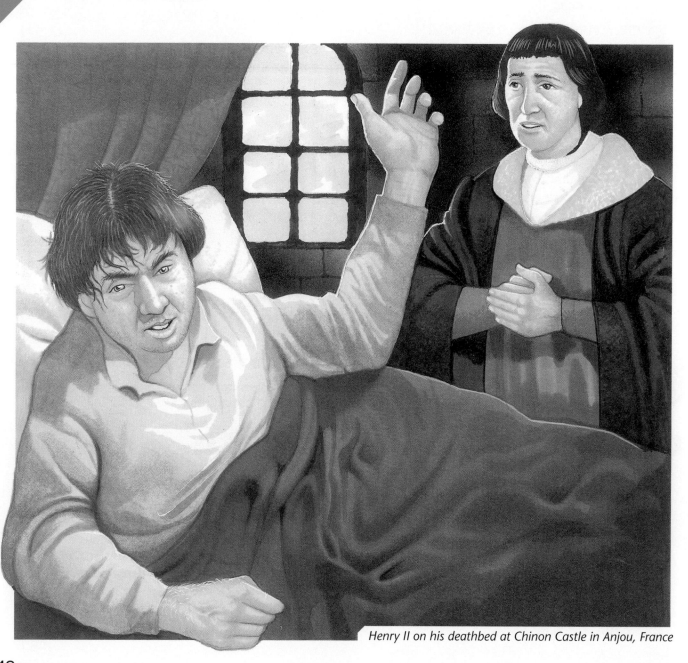

Henry II on his deathbed at Chinon Castle in Anjou, France

On 6 July 1189, Henry II, the first **Angevin** King of England lay dying in Chinon Castle in Anjou, France. He had spent his whole life protecting and expanding his empire, but for what? His eldest surviving son, Richard, joined King Philip II of France to fight against him. They were supported by Henry's wife, Eleanor of Aquitaine. Even his favourite son, John, was with them.

Already ill and old beyond his 56 years, his spirit was broken. His life's work was crumbling around him. He no longer had the energy or the will to fight. He died cursing his sons. He had failed.

And yet an ambassador representing the most powerful emperor in Europe had arrived in England in 1176 to see the man called 'the greatest and most **illustrious** ruler of the world'.

So, what went wrong? Was Henry's kingship really a failure? Perhaps he had made just one or two mistakes? Perhaps he was just unlucky at the end? Could he have been a successful king?

Finding out about Henry

'Hello! It's Brother Thomas again. I've just been given a very difficult task by the abbot. Henry II has just died and I have to write a chronicle of his reign. Some people think he was a strong and successful king. Others think he was a complete failure. I really don't know, but I'm going to investigate and try to decide. I could really do with some help with finding out just how successful he was. I'll find all the information and you can help me to make a judgement of his reign.'

NEW WORDS

Angevin
a person from Anjou, a region in France

Illustrious
well-known and admired person

Henry's early life

Henry II was born at Le Mans in Maine, France on 4 March 1133. His parents were Geoffrey, Count of Anjou and Matilda, Queen of England. Henry was brought up in the households of his father in Anjou and of his uncle, Earl Robert of Gloucester in England. He was very well educated and loved reading. He probably spoke every language used between England and the Holy Land, except English! His great passion was hunting.

As a future leader, Henry II was trained in war and was knighted at the age of 16. In 1149 he landed in England with a small force of **mercenaries**. He was making a claim to the English throne against King Stephen. He avoided capture by Stephen's army and convinced many English nobles that he was worth supporting.

The following year, Henry was made Duke of Normandy and successfully fought off the military attacks of the French king, Louis VII. In 1151, on the death of his father, Henry also became Duke of Anjou. He now controlled much of France and was a powerful leader.

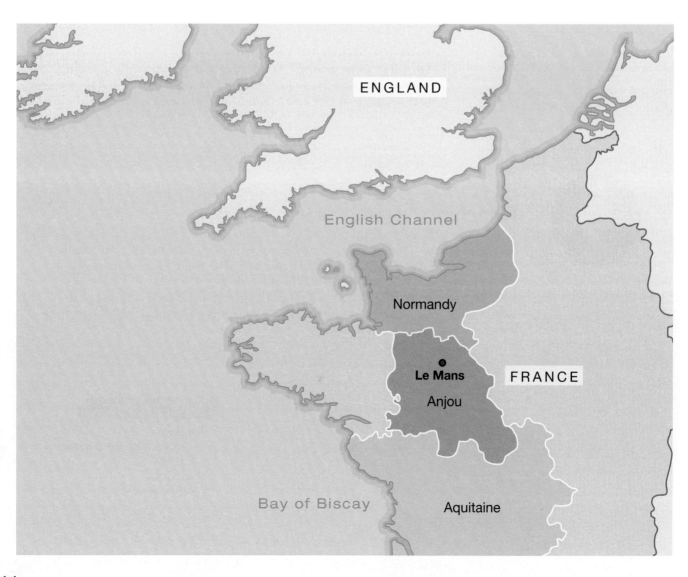

Henry's marriage

In 1152 Henry married Eleanor of Aquitaine. Eleanor had already been married to the King of France. The French king had divorced her, because he wanted a son and she had only given him daughters. She married Henry only six weeks later! Eleanor owned large amounts of land in the south of France. So the marriage extended Henry's empire and meant he controlled nearly as much of France as King Louis VII did.

In 1153 Henry II returned to England with an army and was very successful. King Stephen agreed to a truce and then made Henry his heir. This ended 18 years of civil war in England. When Henry became king in 1154, he was regarded as the only legitimate heir and was widely supported by barons and peasants alike.

Finding out about Henry

'As Henry has just become King of England, you can't help me decide whether or not he is successful yet! But, from what you now know of Henry's early life, do you think he could become a successful monarch? Here are some questions to help you:

- is he from a powerful and respected family?
- will he be able to win arguments with his barons?
- will he be able to lead men in battle?
- has he married wisely?

Write a sentence or two for each of your answers – you'll need them later.'

Henry becomes king

Henry and Eleanor were crowned King and Queen of England at Westminster Abbey in December 1154 by Archbishop Theobald. Between them they controlled an enormous empire.

But England would not be easy to govern. Although everyone accepted that Henry was the rightful king, he had been brought up in Anjou and had spent very little time in England. He spoke only basic English and needed a translator. He did not really understand how English government worked. He also faced a number of very serious problems, which were the result of 30 years of civil war. The success of his kingship would depend on his ability to solve these problems.

SOURCE A

A portrait of Henry II

ACTIVITIES

1. Think about the problems Henry faced. Using the information on page 47, complete this table.

Henry's role	Problem
Policeman	
Judge	
Defender of the empire	
Protector of the Church	

2. Which problem do you think was the most difficult to solve?

3. Which problem do you think Henry dealt with first?

The barons are used to having their own way. How am I going to get them to obey me and the law of the land?

What shall I do about all the '**bastard castles**'? There are over a thousand and they could be used as bases for rebellion.

There is a problem with our neighbours. The Welsh and Scots both seized some of our border lands during the civil war. We must recover it.

There is no justice in the land and the laws are ignored.

There are problems with the King of France, Duke of Brittany, Count of Flanders and barons in Aquitaine. They are claiming some of our territory.

It's a great pity King Stephen lost much of his power over the Church. Now it can appoint its own bishops and try its own people when they break the law of the land, even if they are murderers and robbers – a real problem.

How are we going to pay for everything that needs doing? The royal treasury is empty.

NEW WORDS

Bastard castles
Unlawful. Built without the Kings permission.

Henry, the policeman

During the civil war between Stephen and Matilda, the barons had become much more powerful. They were a real threat to Henry. He decided that his first task must be to deal with the barons.

Luckily, most people in the country co-operated with Henry because he was the undisputed heir. They wanted peace. Also many of the earls who had supported Stephen died in the years 1152 and 1153. This meant many of his enemies had disappeared.

What the barons did

Some of the barons held trials, imposed heavy fines and kept the money for themselves. Most barons hired mercenary soldiers from the continent to fight for them.

Many of them built 'bastard' castles. These were illegal castles, built without the king's permission. They were built to protect the barons in the civil war and to make them more powerful. There were over a thousand of these castles.

One baron, Hugh Mortimer actively resisted Henry. He was the strongest of the **Welsh Marcher Lords**. He made his castles stronger.

NEW WORDS

Keep
strongest tower of a castle

Scuttage
tax paid to the king instead of providing knights to fight for him

Siege
an attempt to force a castle or town to surrender by surrounding it and cutting off supplies

Welsh Marcher Lord
lords on the Welsh borders, given land and power for keeping the peace and controlling the area

How Henry dealt with the problem

Henry ordered all the mercenaries to leave the country – or they would be put in prison. Most quickly went home!

He destroyed nearly 1,000 'bastard' castles in England and became famous as a taker of castles. In 1155 alone, over 300 illegal castles were pulled down. He used mercenary soldiers, specially trained and equipped for **siege** warfare, to capture the castles. These soldiers were paid for by the **Scuttage** tax. All the barons could do was build stronger castles. That cost more money and very few could afford it.

Henry made an example of Hugh Mortimer. When Hugh refused to surrender control of his castles, Henry reacted swiftly and violently. His army laid siege to the castles. They were destroyed and Hugh was forced to swear loyalty to the king in Bridgnorth, in front of most of the barons.

Finally, Henry built his own castles in both England and France. He also improved existing ones. For example, stone **keeps** were added. The keep at Newcastle was built between 1172 and 1177 and cost about £1,000. The one at Dover was built between 1180 and 1190 at a cost of £4,000. These royal castles were safe from the sort of attack the barons could make. They helped Henry to keep control.

Hugh Mortimer swearing loyalty to Henry (artist's interpretation)

Finding out about Henry

'Henry was kept quite busy dealing with his barons, wasn't he? But how successful was he as a policeman?'

'Plot your opinion on a graph like the one on this page. If you think Henry was successful as a policeman, plot an 'x' in the range +1 to +5 above 'Policeman', depending on how successful you think he was. If you think Henry was unsuccessful, put your 'x' in the range -1 to -5. To help you get started, I think he was very successful, so I have plotted my 'x' at +4.

Here are some pointers to help you make up your mind.

- Was Henry right to order all the barons' mercenaries to leave the country?
- Was he right to use mercenaries himself?
- Was he right to destroy the 'bastard' castles?
- Should he have made an example of Hugh Mortimer?
- Why do you think Henry was known as a castle builder?
- Is there anything else he should have done?

You will need to add to your graph again. You also have to be able to explain your decisions, so make notes to keep as you go along.'

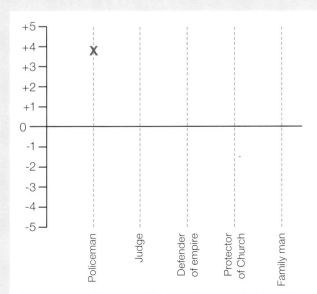

Henry, the judge
The legal system

When Henry became king, he swore that he would make sure there was justice for all his subjects. However, he inherited a legal system that was very unfair and muddled.

Study the diagram to see how the legal system worked.

Manor courts
- were controlled by barons
- barons kept the money from fines for themselves
- often kept the land of those who were executed
- some barons were very greedy

Church courts
- were controlled by the Church
- priests were tried in these courts
- sentences were lighter than under **Canon law**
- some priests literally got away with murder
- known as 'benefit of clergy'

Legal system in 1154

Royal courts
- were controlled by the king
- were held wherever the king was
- few serious crimes were tried in them

NEW WORDS

Canon law
Church law

Hundred
a part of a county or shire, with its own court

Trial by Ordeal
a person's guilt or innocence was tested by a painful or dangerous ordeal. such as being thrown into deep water or holding a burning hot iron bar.

How Henry dealt with the problem

Henry ruled a large empire and could not be everywhere at once. He needed a strong system to keep order. So gradually he introduced a new system, which is explained in this diagram.

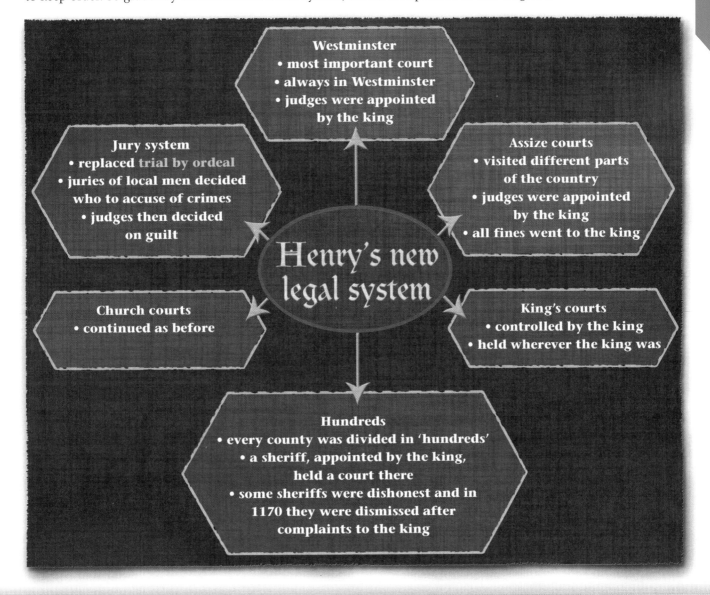

Westminster
- most important court
- always in Westminster
- judges were appointed by the king

Jury system
- replaced trial by ordeal
- juries of local men decided who to accuse of crimes
- judges then decided on guilt

Assize courts
- visited different parts of the country
- judges were appointed by the king
- all fines went to the king

Henry's new legal system

Church courts
- continued as before

King's courts
- controlled by the king
- held wherever the king was

Hundreds
- every county was divided in 'hundreds'
- a sheriff, appointed by the king, held a court there
- some sheriffs were dishonest and in 1170 they were dismissed after complaints to the king

Finding out about Henry

'Henry made lots of changes to the legal system, didn't he? But do you think he gave all his subjects justice? Just how successful do you think he was as a judge? Plot your opinion on your graph. Remember, you have to be able to justify it! Here are some pointers to help you.

1. What main change to the legal system did Henry introduce?

2. Which parts of the legal system stayed the same after Henry's reforms?

3. In what ways do you think Henry's reforms improved the legal system?

4. Are there any ways in which the reforms made the system worse?

5. Do you think it was possible to get a fair trial after Henry's changes?'

Henry, the defender of empire

Henry II's empire was known as the Angevin Empire. This name was given to all the lands of the Counts of Anjou during the time they ruled England.

The empire was very large. As a result, Henry was always on the move. He crossed the English Channel at least 28 times during the 35 years of his reign. It was a dangerous crossing.

NEW WORDS

Diplomacy
  working out problems without fighting
Dowry
  payment to a husband on marriage
Overlord
  ruler of lords

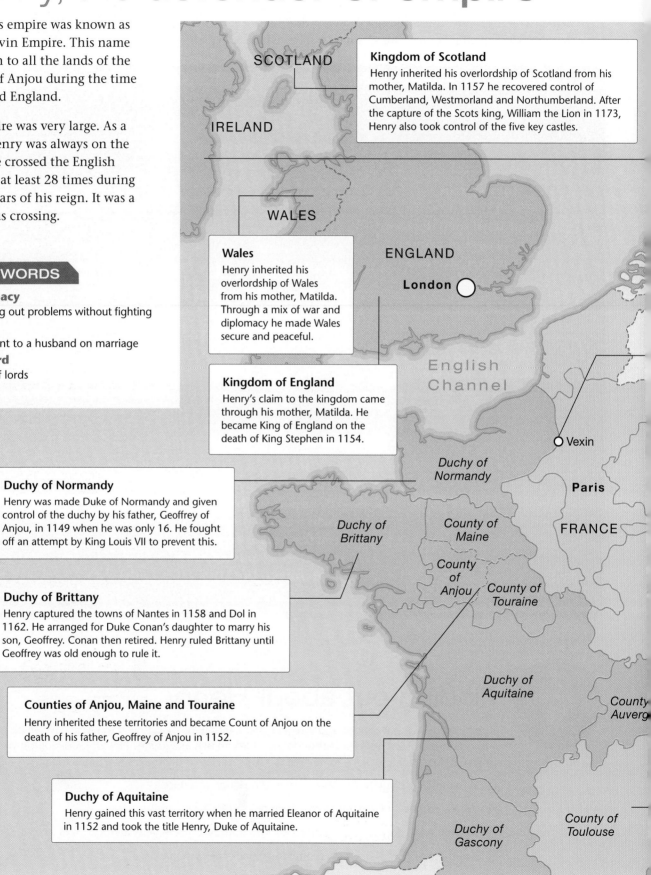

Kingdom of Scotland
Henry inherited his overlordship of Scotland from his mother, Matilda. In 1157 he recovered control of Cumberland, Westmorland and Northumberland. After the capture of the Scots king, William the Lion in 1173, Henry also took control of the five key castles.

Wales
Henry inherited his overlordship of Wales from his mother, Matilda. Through a mix of war and diplomacy he made Wales secure and peaceful.

Kingdom of England
Henry's claim to the kingdom came through his mother, Matilda. He became King of England on the death of King Stephen in 1154.

Duchy of Normandy
Henry was made Duke of Normandy and given control of the duchy by his father, Geoffrey of Anjou, in 1149 when he was only 16. He fought off an attempt by King Louis VII to prevent this.

Duchy of Brittany
Henry captured the towns of Nantes in 1158 and Dol in 1162. He arranged for Duke Conan's daughter to marry his son, Geoffrey. Conan then retired. Henry ruled Brittany until Geoffrey was old enough to rule it.

Counties of Anjou, Maine and Touraine
Henry inherited these territories and became Count of Anjou on the death of his father, Geoffrey of Anjou in 1152.

Duchy of Aquitaine
Henry gained this vast territory when he married Eleanor of Aquitaine in 1152 and took the title Henry, Duke of Aquitaine.

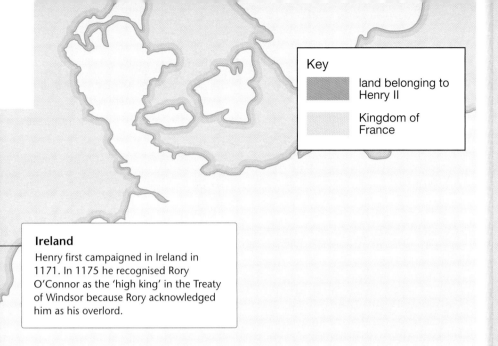

Ireland

Henry first campaigned in Ireland in 1171. In 1175 he recognised Rory O'Connor as the 'high king' in the Treaty of Windsor because Rory acknowledged him as his overlord.

Vexin

Henry gained this land as the **dowry** of Margaret of France, who was engaged to his son and heir, Henry. Henry II moved in and took control in 1160.

Kingdom of France

The territories under the control of Louis VII, who was both Henry II's **overlord** and his main rival in France.

County of Toulouse

Henry claimed these lands, but he failed to take them by force in 1159. However, in 1173 the Count of Toulouse made **homage** to Henry for his lands and so acknowledged Henry as his overlord.

Map of the British Isles and France in the period 1150–80

Finding out about Henry

'It's time to decide just how successful Henry was at defending his empire. As before, plot your opinion on your graph. The following pointers might help you come to your decision.

- Which lands did Henry inherit or gain peacefully through marriage?
- Which lands did Henry gain through war?
- Which lands did Henry gain by a mix of peaceful and warlike means?
- With which states was Henry most likely to find himself at war?
- Was Henry successful at keeping and controlling the territories he gained?
- Was Henry too greedy or ambitious?

Remember to note down your reasons as you will need them later.'

NEW WORDS

Homage
Acknowledging someone as lord

Henry, the **protector of the Church**

'The rider was tired. He had been in the saddle for four days. He had eaten nothing but bread and he had drunk only water. Now, from the top of a hill, he could see the end of his journey only a few miles away – the cathedral in the city of Canterbury.

But he did not spur his horse to finish the journey quickly. He dismounted, took off his clothes and shoes, and put on a shirt lined with stiff, prickly hair. Then, leaving his horse, he began walking barefoot into the city.

The road was rough and stony, and his feet were soon bleeding. As he entered the cathedral he left footprints of blood behind him. Painfully, he walked downstairs into the crypt, a burial place beneath the cathedral floor. There, he knelt before the tomb of a man who had been murdered several years before, and wept.

As he did so, eighty monks filed into the crypt behind him. Each was carrying a whip. The man took off his hair shirt and, one by one, the monks whipped his bare back with three lashes each.

When they had finished, the man dressed and stayed the night alone in the dark, cold crypt. He left the cathedral early in the morning, taking with him some small bottles of holy water, mixed with blood from the body in the tomb.

The man's name was Henry and he was the King of England.
The body was that of Thomas Becket. The year was 1174.'

From Thomas Becket, Saint or Troublemaker? *By Josh Brooman*

SOURCE B

Henry II doing **penance** *at the tomb of Thomas Becket*

Can you imagine a king as strong as Henry II
doing penance? So what was it all about?
Why did this happen?

The background

Thomas Becket was born in London in 1118. He was the son of wealthy Norman parents. He was tall, dark and handsome, and very charming and witty. He was also very ambitious. He worked as a lawyer, a merchant and then as an assistant to Theobald, the Archbishop of Canterbury.

When King Stephen died, the new king, Henry II, wanted different people to work for him. On Theobald's advice, he appointed Thomas as Chancellor in 1155. Thomas was 37. The Chancellor was the king's closest adviser. He went everywhere with the king, dealt with his letters and kept records of his finances.

For seven years he did the job very well and they became good friends. Thomas was richly rewarded and he bought lots of luxuries. His clothes were made of silk and fur, his horses were harnessed with silver, he showered his friends with gifts and entertained them lavishly. He went hunting, **hawking** and riding with the king and they played chess together.

Then in 1161 Theobald died and Henry wanted Thomas to replace him.

NEW WORDS

Hawking
hunting with a hawk

Penance
Punishment for a sin

ACTIVITIES

1. Why do you think Henry wanted Thomas to become Archbishop of Canterbury? (Clue: look back at the sections on Henry becoming king and Henry, the judge.)

2. In what ways was Thomas suited to the position?

3. In what ways wasn't he suited to the position?

4. Do you think it was a good idea to make him Archbishop of Canterbury?

The quarrel

The story really begins when Thomas finally agreed to become Archbishop of Canterbury in 1162. From then on his relationship with Henry changed. They started to disagree about everything. Thomas became a different person. He no longer went hunting and hawking with the king. Sometimes he prayed all night. In 1163 he resigned as Chancellor.

Henry wanted Thomas to help him regain some of the power King Stephen had given away to the Church. He wanted Thomas to reduce the power of the Church courts. He thought it was wrong that sentences were much lighter under Canon law than in the king's courts. But now Thomas believed he had to protect the power of the Church. His master was no longer Henry, but God. He also had to convince the Church that he was his own man and not the king's puppet.

The first major clash came in 1163. Henry wanted to deal with the problem of 'criminal clerks'. Anyone who had been educated by the Church could claim to be a 'clerk in minor orders' and tried in Church courts. Henry wanted to change this, but Thomas refused to agree. He saw it as an attack on the power of the Church. He then upset Henry further by **excommunicating** a baron from the Church without the king's permission.

In 1164 Henry wanted all serious Church court cases to be tried again in the king's courts. At first Thomas and all the bishops refused to agree. Then without talking to his bishops, Thomas gave in – but changed his mind again later. Henry was furious and so were the bishops.

Soon afterwards Henry accused Thomas of misusing royal money when he was Chancellor. Thomas guessed that he was in danger and ran away to France. Some of the bishops tried to persuade Thomas to come to an agreement. They thought the quarrel was harming the Church. But Thomas refused.

In 1169 Henry and Thomas met in France. The meeting was intended to make the peace between them, but it failed.

Thomas Becket is made Archbishop

King Henry II and Thomas Becket arguing

Thomas responded by excommunicating several of the king's closest advisers, including the bishops of London and Salisbury. So Henry ordered the Archbishop of York instead of Thomas to crown his son, Henry 'the Young King' as the next King of England. Thomas was very angry, but it persuaded him to talk to Henry again.

So in July 1170 Thomas and Henry met in France. This time they patched up their quarrel and Thomas returned to England. Henry remained in Normandy. Almost immediately Thomas excommunicated several of the bishops who had supported Henry against him and asked the Pope to punish the Archbishop of York.

Some of those bishops went to France and told Henry what Thomas was doing. Henry was furious. In a rage he shouted, 'Will no one rid me of this meddlesome priest?' Four knights took Henry at his word and set off for England. Henry soon calmed down. When he was told that the knights had gone, he guessed they might harm Thomas to try to please him. He sent messengers to stop them, but it was too late!

Thomas Becket sails to France

Thomas Becket excommunicates his enemies

NEW WORDS

Excommunicating
throwing someone out of the Church

The crime

We are very lucky to have an eyewitness account for this part of the story. Edward Grim was a priest who was with Thomas at the time. He was also wounded. Read his account of what happened in Source C.

SOURCE C

'The murderers came in full armour, with swords and axes. The monks cried out to the Archbishop to flee … They pulled, dragged and pushed him into the cathedral. The four knights followed with rapid strides. The archbishop ordered the doors of the cathedral to be kept open.

In a spirit of mad fury the knights called out, 'Where is Thomas Becket, traitor to the king and to the country?' At this, he quite unafraid came down the steps and answered 'Here I am, no traitor to the king, but a priest.'

'You shall die this instant,' they cried.

Becket inclined his head as in prayer and joined his hands together and uplifted them. The wicked knight (William Fitz Urse) leapt suddenly upon him and wounded him in the head.

Next he received a second blow on the head (struck by William de Traci), but still he stood firm.

At the third blow he fell on his knees and elbows, saying in a low voice, 'For the name of Jesus I am ready to die.'

The next blow (struck by Richard Brito) separated the crown of his head and the blood white with brain and the brain red with blood stained the floor.

The fourth knight (Hugh of Morville) warded off any who sought to interfere.

A fifth man (Hugh of Horsea) placed his foot on the neck of the holy priest and scattered the brains and blood about the pavement, crying out to the others, 'Let us away, knights; this fellow will rise no more.'

Written by the priest, Edward Grim

ACTIVITIES

1. List all the adjectives (describing words) you can find that Edward Grim used to make the knights look bad.

2. List all the adjectives you can find that he used to make Thomas look good.

3. Does this mean that Edward Grim is an unreliable witness?

4. Now look at Source D. In what ways does it agree with Source C? In what ways does it disagree with Source C?

5. Do Sources C and D together tell us what happened in Canterbury Cathedral?

A painting from about 1190 showing the murder of Thomas Becket and Edward Grim trying to protect him with a cross

What happened afterwards

When Henry heard about the murder, he was overcome with grief. He shut himself away for three days. His friends feared for his health and sanity. The Pope did not believe that Henry had ordered the murder, but Henry admitted that his anger had led to Becket's death. For the rest of his reign, Henry enjoyed good relations with the Church.

NEW WORDS

Traitor
person who goes against the king

Finding out about Henry

'Now you need to decide how successful Henry was in his dealings with the Church. Plot your opinion on your graph and don't forget your notes as before. Here are some pointers to help you make your decision.

- Do you think the quarrel was personal or about power over the Church?
- If it was personal, do you think Henry acted wisely?
- If it was about power, do you think Henry's actions were sensible?
- What could Henry have done differently?

Remember that Thomas Becket was murdered and that he was strong-willed. Remember Henry's relations with the Church improved after Becket's death.'

Henry, the **family man**

Henry had spent his whole life protecting and expanding his empire. He had been described as 'the greatest and most illustrious ruler of the world'. Yet, as he lay dying in Chinon Castle in Anjou in July 1189, his life's work seemed to crumble around him …

Henry II

'Everything's been for the sake of my family. My wife, Eleanor was the Duchess of Aquitaine. Together our lands created a large empire. At first she was a great support to me and even acted as **regent** in England when I had to be out of the country. Our eldest son died very young but four others reached adulthood. But Eleanor is very wilful and she does not always behave like a queen. She encouraged my sons to rebel against me in 1173, so I had to put her in prison.

My sons were the reason I worked so hard defending and extending my empire. I wanted them all to inherit my land. My eldest, Henry, was crowned King of England and Duke of Normandy, but he was lazy and vain, and he spent his time gambling. I even forgave him after his rebellion in 1173 and gave him more responsibility, but he died in 1183.

I made my third son, Geoffrey, the Duke of Brittany. He was bright, but he was also devious and foolish. He liked taking part in tournaments and was trampled to death at one in Paris in 1186.

Richard, my second son, was always Eleanor's favourite. He's very impatient. Since 1172 he's been the Duke of Aquitaine. He's been demanding that I name him as my heir in England, Normandy and Anjou. Eleanor and Philip II of France have supported him. They have just rebelled against me again and beaten me – but I pray God I can take my revenge!

John, my youngest son, has always been my favourite. I made him King of Ireland in 1177, but he changed that to Lord of Ireland. Now my courtiers tell me he joined Richard against me. I just can't believe it!'

NEW WORDS

Illegitimate
person born when their parents are not married

Regent
person who rules until a king is old enough to rule for himself

---

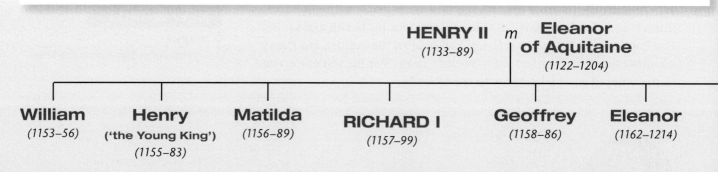

HENRY II *m* **Eleanor of Aquitaine**
(1133–89)   (1122–1204)

William	**Henry** ('the Young King')	**Matilda**	**RICHARD I**	**Geoffrey**	**Eleanor**
(1153–56)	(1155–83)	(1156–89)	(1157–99)	(1158–86)	(1162–1214)

Richard

'I'm Henry II's second son. Since my elder brother died, I should be heir to the Angevin Empire, but father favours my brother John. Mother sticks up for me, so he made me Duke of Aquitaine in 1171, but never gave me any real power. He treated my brothers Henry and Geoffrey the same! No wonder we rebelled in 1173. He makes me so mad! It's even rumoured that he's sleeping with my intended bride, Alais, the French princess. And although we've just beaten him, he's still refusing to name me as his heir. Well, let him suffer like I have!'

Eleanor

'I've been married to Henry since 1152. I grew up in Aquitaine and, on the death of my brother in 1130, I became heiress to the duchy and the most valuable marriage partner in Europe. I had a formal education and inherited Aquitaine in 1137. I was just 15. Shortly afterwards I married King Louis VII of France. We had two lovely daughters. I even went with him on the Second Crusade in 1147. But in 1152 he divorced me because I hadn't given him a son.

Six weeks later I married Henry. I was so much in love with him. I ruled England for him while he was in France. Although we had eight children, he still went chasing after other women. As far as I know, he's had at least 12 **illegitimate** children. Is it surprising that I prefer to spend my time in Aquitaine? He won't give any real power to my sons. No wonder they go against him. And I've helped them. I shan't shed any tears when he's gone.'

| Joan | JOHN |
| (1165–99) | (1167–1216) |

John

'I'm Henry II`s youngest son. I'm supposed to be his favourite, but I can't say I've noticed. He made me King of Ireland in 1177, but it means nothing. I had no real power – just like my brothers. He's been going to give me some of Richard's land, but it won't make any difference. I still won't have any power. So I joined Richard's rebellion.'

Finding out about Henry

'Have you noticed how Henry's interpretation of events is very different from his family's? It's going to be very difficult to decide how successful he was as a family man to complete your graph. Perhaps these questions will help you to reach your decision.

- Why did Henry think he was a good father?
- Why didn't Eleanor agree?
- Why didn't his sons agree?

Now think about the following statements. Decide which ones you agree with and why.

- Henry was successful because he had male heirs.
- Henry was unsuccessful because he had too many sons.
- Henry gave his sons too much power.
- Henry gave his sons too little power.
- Henry shouldn't have tried to divide his lands between his sons.
- Henry shouldn't have treated Eleanor so badly. Then she wouldn't have encouraged her sons to rebel.

Complete your graph and remember to note down your ideas.'

Writing your chronicle

'Henry packed a great deal into his 56 years, didn't he? But the big question we have to answer for our chronicle was – how successful was Henry II?

We've got all the information now. By breaking the big question down into smaller questions on the graph, we've also done a lot of the thinking too. You just need to write the chronicle! Remember to support your opinions with lots of detail. Here's a plan to check you don't forget anything important.'

Plan	Focus	Source of evidence
Introduction	Could Henry be successful?	One paragraph based on Henry's early life and becoming king.
Main part of the chronicle	How successful was he?	Paragraph 1, based on Henry, the policeman. Paragraph 2, based on Henry, the judge. Paragraph 3, based on Henry, the defender of empire Paragraph 4, based on Henry, the protector of the Church Paragraph 5, based on Henry, the family man.
Conclusion		Paragraph pulling all your ideas together. Overall, how successful was he? What were his strengths? What were his weaknesses? How should we remember him?

| 1189 | 1190 | | 1200 | | 1210 | 1215 |

1189
King Henry II dies and Richard I becomes king

1199
John becomes king when Richard I dies fighting in France

1215
Magna Carta is signed

The signing of Magna Carta

What was great about Magna Carta?

In June 1215, King John and many of his barons met at Runnymede, near the River Thames, to try to sort out their arguments.

When John became king in 1199, the royal treasury was empty. King Richard had spent all the money on his crusade. So John had to raise taxes to pay for running the country. John was also greedy. He wanted lots of money for himself. So taxes went up again. And John had to fight many wars because the Kings of France and Scotland tried to get back the lands they had lost to Henry II. These wars cost a lot of money – so taxes went up yet again. If John had won the wars, it would not have

SOURCE A

The Magna Carta

mattered so much, but he kept losing and became very unpopular. At last, the barons would take no more – it looked like there would be civil war.

In an attempt to prevent war, the Archbishop of Canterbury suggested the barons write down their demands. Then they should discuss them with the king and come to a sensible agreement. Magna Carta was the result.

SOURCE B

Key points of Magna Carta

- The king must not interfere with the Church.

- When a baron inherited land, he had to pay the king the traditional price of £100 (John had been demanding £5,000 or £6,000).

- Widows should not be forced to re-marry (John was raising money by fining widows who wished to remain single).

- The king must not demand taxes or other payment without the permission of the barons and bishops.

- No free man should be arrested or imprisoned without a fair trial.

- The king would release all hostages he had taken from the barons.

- All foreign mercenaries would be sent home.

- The barons would appoint 25 barons to make certain the king kept to the terms of Magna Carta.

The signing of the Magna Carta an early 20th Century painting

What was the significance of Magna Carta?

At the time, nobody really expected Magna Carta to keep the peace, even though the Archbishop of Canterbury hoped it might. The barons didn't trust King John and he really did not want to surrender any of his power. In fact, within four months they were fighting again. The barons even invited Prince Louis, the son of the King of France, to come over and they offered him the throne.

However, Magna Carta is one of those events in history that are thought to be very important, or significant. People interpret such events in a way that suits their own ideas and Magna Carta has been seen in different ways at different times.

- In the 1640s, when **Parliament** was quarrelling with King Charles I over who should run the country, Parliament used Magna Carta to support its claim for more power.

- In 1776, when the American **colonies** were fighting for their independence, some parts of Magna Carta were included in the American **Constitution** to support the colonies' claim to be free from the King of England.

- In Victorian times, when many people wanted **democracy**, Magna Carta was said to be the origin of Parliament because it limited the queen's right to rule alone.

- After World War II, a war 'fought for freedom from **tyranny**', Magna Carta was used as the basis for the Universal Declaration of Human Rights, a document that set out everyone's rights and freedoms.

NEW WORDS

Colonies
countries controlled by another country

Constitution
rules and guidelines for governing a state

Democracy
type of government in which ordinary people vote and have some power

Parliament
body of elected representatives responsible for running a country

Tyranny
cruelty

ACTIVITIES

1. What did the barons gain from Magna Carta in 1215? (Clue: look at the list of key points.)

2. What was the significance of Magna Carta for King John in 1215?

3. Why has Magna Carta been so important since 1215?

4. What was 'great' about Magna Carta?

SOURCE C

American Lawyers' Memorial to Magna Carta

1215	1220	1230	1240	1250

1215	Oct 1215	1216	1238	1267
Magna Carta is signed	Siege of Rochester Castle begins	Colchester, Framlingham and Hedingham all surrender to King John	Eleanor marries Simon de Montfort, Earl of Leicester	Henry III makes Prince Llewelyn Prince of Wales

1215 – 1295

How and why did castles change?

Of pickaxes and pigs

On 14 October 1215, King John gave this order to the men of Canterbury:

> 'We order you ... to make by day and night all the pickaxes you can. Every blacksmith in your city should stop all other work in order to make [them] ... and you should send them to us at Rochester with all speed.'

Blacksmiths at work

On 25 November 1215, John sent this letter to his trusted servant, Sir Hubert de Burgh:

> 'We order you to send us forty bacon pigs ... the fattest and least good for eating.'

Why did King John want pickaxes and pigs? Perhaps the answer is surprising – he was planning to break into Rochester Castle.

The background

This story begins shortly after the signing of Magna Carta. The barons quickly realised that King John had no intention of keeping his promises. They decided to offer the crown to Prince Louis, the eldest son of the King of France, and they prepared for war. The king also looked across the Channel for support, but from mercenaries. He and his army marched to the south coast to make sure the Channel ports were loyal and to wait for the mercenaries to arrive. The rebel barons made their headquarters in London and planned to stop King John and his army returning to the city. So control of Rochester Castle, which stood where the main road to London crossed the River Medway, became all important.

> **At the end of this unit you are going to produce a brochure for Beaumaris Castle. All the activities in the unit will help you with this final task.**

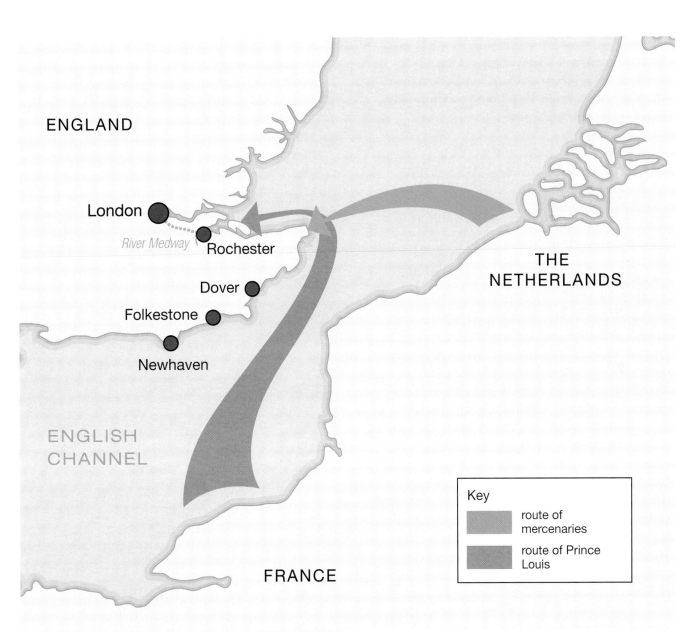

ENGLAND

London

River Medway · Rochester

Dover

Folkestone

Newhaven

THE NETHERLANDS

ENGLISH CHANNEL

FRANCE

Key

route of mercenaries

route of Prince Louis

Map of southeast England, France and the Netherlands in 1215

The siege of Rochester Castle

Rochester's **constable**, Sir Reginald de Cornhill, supported the rebels and allowed them to occupy the castle. A detachment of knights, led by Sir William de Albini, prepared to defend it against King John. In just two days they stocked the castle with enough ammunition, weapons and food to withstand an attack or a siege.

On 11 October, the king's army surprised the rebels by destroying the bridge leading into Rochester. Then they surrounded the castle. Help from London could no longer get through to the rebels.

King John arrived on 13 October. He immediately ordered that five siege engines be set up. They hurled rocks at the castle non-stop for a number of days. His knights attacked the castle, using battering rams and siege towers, and his archers and crossbowmen shot at anyone who appeared on the castle walls. On 14 October, King John sent his urgent message to Canterbury for pickaxes, which were needed by the miners for digging tunnels under the walls.

The **besieged** rebels threw stones and fired arrows from the walls and ramparts, killing many royal troops. According to the chronicle written by Matthew Paris, a monk from St Albans, King John was nearly killed by a crossbow. Before the crossbowman let his arrow fly at the king, he asked Sir William de Albini for permission. The rebel leader refused, saying that it was for God, not men, to end the lives of kings.

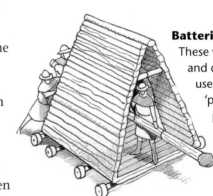

Battering rams
These were used to smash walls and doors. They were often used with mobile sheds called 'penthouses' or 'sows', which protected the men using the ram.

Crossbowmen
Crossbows were slow to load but deadly accurate. They were perfect for firing through the narrow slits in castle walls.

Archers
They used the traditional English longbow, which was rapid to fire and effective over longer distances – a perfect attacking weapon.

Siege engines
Stones were repeatedly thrown from these engines. They concentrated on the same parts of the walls, which eventually weakened and fell down.

Siege towers
Some towers were pushed up to the castle walls on wheels. A drawbridge on the tower was then lowered so the attackers could get onto the walls. Other towers stood away from the walls to provide a better place from which to shoot arrows into the castle.

Scaling ladders
Attackers used these ladders to climb to the top of castle walls.

Tunnels
Miners tunnelled under the walls of the castle to weaken them. The tunnel roofs were held up by wooden props. When the miners reached the walls, they set the props on fire and the walls above collapsed.

The siege continued for some weeks. The siege engines could not break through the walls and scaling ladders could not reach the top. Meanwhile the miners continued to tunnel. When they reached the castle walls, the tunnel was packed with brushwood, straw and kindling, and set alight. When the walls collapsed, the king's army stormed the castle. Most of the rebels headed for the strongest building, a keep that was 34 metres high with walls 4 metres thick.

King John's miners tunnelled under the corners of the keep. Then the king sent his unusual order for 40 pigs, which were killed and melted down. The fat was probably poured into barrels, which were placed in the tunnels and set alight. As the fire grew, the southeast corner of the keep collapsed and the king's men charged in.

Even this was not the end for the rebels. The inside of the keep was divided by a strong wall. The rebels retreated behind it and kept the king's men out. But although they had water, they had no food. They had to kill their horses to survive. When that meat ran out, they had no choice but to surrender.

It had taken King John nearly two months to take Rochester Castle. The rebels elsewhere were very discouraged. When the king attacked Colchester, Framlingham and Hedingham Castles in the spring of 1216, they quickly surrendered.

NEW WORDS

Besieged
  to be surrounded in a castle by attackers wanting its surrender
Constable
  person in charge of a castle and responsible to the lord for its safety

Finding out about castles

1 If you had only a few days to prepare Rochester Castle for a siege, what items would you take into the castle? Why?

2 Why did the barons think Rochester Castle was a good place to stop King John?

3 Why did the siege last so long?

4 What defensive features of Rochester Castle made it so strong?

5 What methods did King John use to capture Rochester Castle?

6 Think about the weaknesses in the design of Rochester Castle that allowed its capture. In what ways do you think the design of castles changed afterwards?

Life at Odiham Castle

At home with the Countess of Leicester

On 19 March 1265, Eleanor the Countess of Leicester and her 60 servants waited at Odiham Castle. They were expecting the arrival of Eleanor's husband, Simon de Montfort, the Earl of Leicester, with over 100 armed knights and many more servants.

The outriders arrived first to make sure everything was ready. Then the earl arrived with his attendants and knights. Finally lots of servants arrived with the hunting dogs, packhorses and carts. They also brought many of the household possessions – the bath, bed, locks, tapestries and much more, as well as a large sum of money.

The castle, often almost empty, was now a hive of activity. Grooms stabled hundreds of horses; cooks prepared food for 200 extra people; livestock, needed for food, roamed around the bailey; servants drew water and arranged household possessions; knights practised their skills; spinners, weavers and embroiderers made clothes; cobblers made shoes, chandlers made candles and billers made axes; coopers built barrels; and blacksmiths hammered at their forges. Imagine the noise and the smell!

Just two weeks later, the earl, his knights and servants moved on, followed on 1 June by Eleanor and her servants. The castle returned to its usual sleepy state.

This pattern was repeated many times a year and not just by the Earl and Countess of Leicester. Other great nobles did the same. They visited friends and relatives. And they had to keep control in their lands, punishing those guilty of crimes, collecting rent and even minting their own coins. For example, in the 34 years of his reign, Henry II spent Christmas in 24 different castles on both sides of the English Channel!

Eleanor, Countess of Leicester

Eleanor was the granddaughter of Henry II and the sister of Henry III. She was married at the age of nine and widowed at 16. She then took a vow of **chastity**, but broke it in January 1238 to marry Simon de Montfort, the Earl of Leicester. Their first child, Henry, was born before the end of 1238.

Like other great nobles, Simon and Eleanor owned vast, scattered estates. They were constantly on the move. Their main castles were at Kenilworth and Odiham. Sometimes Eleanor accompanied Simon on his travels on both sides of the English Channel. When Simon went on crusade to the Holy Land in 1240, she travelled as far as southern Italy with him, despite being pregnant. More often, she ran the household and their estates while he was away on business.

NEW WORDS

Chastity
to never have sex or marry

The Countess' account books

We are very lucky that some of the Countess of Leicester's account books have survived. Here are some extracts from her accounts for part of 1265.

SOURCE A

25 April	Ale, by purchase, 188 gallons, 7s 3d; Fish, bought, 8s 6d; Stable hay for 31 horses
26 April	For the kitchen 1½ oxen; 3 sheep 16s, calves, 3s 3d
28 April	For the kitchen ½ ox from the castle stores; 1 sheep and 1 calf, 3s 3d; 500 eggs, 1s 5½d; milk, 1d; 3 quarters of grain for 46 dogs
30 April	2lbs cinnamon for making sauce, 2s; 1lb cloves, 14s
2 May	300 herring from the castle stores; 600 eggs, 1s 10½d
3 May	For 4 geese bought, 1s 4d; 12lbs sugar, 12s
4 May	Grain for the poor for 8 days, ½ quarter and 13 gallons ale; grain for the dogs for 10 days, 3 quarters.
6 May	Fish, 6s 11d; calf, 1s; 400 eggs, 1s 3d; cheese for tarts, 9d
7 May	1 ox and 1 sheep, 7s; hens, 2s 6d; 300 eggs, 11¼d; wax, 13 lbs; pepper for the foals, ½lb, 5d; 6lbs of ginger, 15s
10 May	For expenses of W the Carter going to Porchester with 3 horses to obtain 1 tun of wine, 3s; given to the barber of Reading for coming twice to Odiham to bleed a damsel, 2s 8d; for baths at Odiham, 3d; for locks for the chests, 2d
31 May	Paid to Hande, the groom from the bakery, dismissed, for 2 years wages, 7s

'Old' money

There were 12 pence (pennies, written as 'd') in 1 shilling (s) and 20 shillings in £1. Of course money was worth a lot more in those days, e.g. a groom's wages for two years was 7s.

Finding out about castles

1. Sort the items in the Countess' account into three groups and enter them in a table like this.

Items grown on the castle estate	Items bought in locally	Items bought from a long way
Ox from castle stores	4 geese bought	2lbs cinnamon

2. What did the people in the castle eat and drink a lot of?

3. What did they eat just a little of?

4. Which foods were most expensive? Which were least expensive?

5. What do you notice about the quantities of food bought and cooked?

6. What did the animals eat?

7. Are there items missing from the list that you think surprising?

8. How did items bought a long way away get to Odiham? How can you tell? Was this expensive?

9. Where did items like cinnamon and ginger come from? They used great quantities of them. Why were they in such demand?

10. How is the diet similar to today, and how is it different?

Inside the castle

Sleeping arrangements

The Earl and Countess of Leicester had private sleeping quarters above the great hall. They were kept warm by the heat from a small fireplace, heavy blankets, feather mattresses, fur covers and wall tapestries. Important guests had chambers of their own. The rest of the household were not so fortunate. Usually they slept where they worked on straw **pallets**, a bench or the floor, covered only by a light blanket. It would have been very cold and dark in winter.

Walls

Tapestries were often hung on the walls. They were used as decorations, but they also blocked out the cold and damp.

Great hall

Everyone ate here. The lord and lady sat at a 'high table', with their children, guests and most important knights and officials. This was on a raised platform, called a dais, at one end of the hall. They were always served first. Everyone else sat on wooden benches at trestle tables down the length of the hall. The tables were often dismantled between meals.

Chapel

This was a very important part of any castle. It was where the lord and his family heard morning **mass** every day. They even had their own priest!

Lighting

During the day, light came into the hall through narrow openings in the walls. These were quite high up and let in the sun, wind, snow and rain. After dark, wooden shutters were drawn across the openings. Candles or rushlights, fixed to spikes on the walls or to an iron ring hanging from the ceiling, were lit.

Floors

Rushes were strewn on floors. They hid all sorts of dirt and food remains, such as animal droppings, grease and bones. The rushes were replaced from time to time.

Entertainment

There was often entertainment at dinner. Jugglers, dancers, acrobats and minstrels playing lutes and harps were all very popular. After dinner the lord and his guests often went hunting.

Food and drink

There were three meals a day. For breakfast there was bread with ale or watered wine. The main meal was a dinner of three or four courses, served mid-morning. Supper was usually eaten quite late, sometimes just before bedtime.

There were no forks, so people used knives and their fingers. Thick slices of stale bread, called trenchers, were used as plates that soaked up the fat from the very greasy food.

The meat was often old, tough and tasteless. It was stored in salt barrels to preserve it and flavoured with popular spices from the East, such as cinnamon, pepper, cloves and ginger. Fortunately there was a well-stocked fishpond at Odiham and the earl and his knights also hunted for venison and game.

The water drawn from the well was not usually fit to drink, so most people drank ale or perhaps cider, and the rich drank wine.

Plumbing

This was very basic. Water was carried into the great hall at meal times for people to wash their hands. They occasionally had baths in a wooden tub.

Toilets, called latrines or 'garderobes', were just holes with chutes for the waste to fall down. They were often built into the thick outside walls over a moat or river so that the waste would be washed away. Chamber pots were also used by the lord, his family and their guests.

Kitchen

This was a separate building to avoid the risk of fire in the keep. Meat was either boiled in a cauldron or roasted on a spit over the fire in the huge fireplace. Bread and pastry were baked in the oven. A fire was lit inside the oven. When the ashes were white hot, they were raked to the side and the dough was pushed in on a pole.

Heating

A very large fireplace, with a hood and a mantle, heated the hall. Smoke escaped through the chimney.

Finding out about castles

1 Think about what it would have been like to live in Odiham Castle.
   a) In what ways would daily life be similar to today?
   b) In what ways would it be different to today?

2 Do you think Odiham Castle was designed for living in or for fighting in? Explain your answer.

3 How and why do you think Odiham Castle was different to Rochester?

4 Imagine you are either the priest or the constable at Odiham Castle. Write a diary entry for 19 March 1265, the day Simon de Montfort and all his men arrived at the castle. Remember, over 200 men needed accommodating. What did they eat and drink? Where did they all sleep? What about washing and toilet facilities? What about all the horses and other animals?

5 Now write a diary entry for two weeks later after they had all left.

6 List as many reasons as you can why households moved on so often.

In defence of honour
at Conway Castle

The seige of Conway Castle

In the winter of 1294 Edward I and 8,000 men were trapped by the Welsh in the town and castle at Conway in northern Wales. It was bitterly cold. Most of the men were living in tents with animals close by. There was no proper **sanitation** and the risk of disease was very great. Supplies were rapidly running out and the English supply lines were cut off. Edward I and his men faced death from cold and starvation.

In the end, they survived and took their revenge. The reason? Edward had chosen to site Conway Castle, like Caernarvon and Harlech Castles, right on the seashore. Ships bringing supplies of grain and vegetables, wine, chicken and fish took a long time to arrive, but when they did they could actually get to the troops. So, after three months in a city of tents, the king's men ended up with more food than they could eat.

But why had all this happened at all and what were its consequences?

NEW WORDS

Sanitation
toilets and sewers

The background

In 1272, Edward became King of England. At the start of his reign, Wales was a completely separate country, ruled by the Marcher Lords and Welsh Princes. They had the power to raise their own taxes and build their own castles, but they did homage to the King of England. During the reign of Edward's father, Henry III, Prince Llewelyn of Gwynedd extended his power over much of Wales. He still paid homage to the King of England and in 1267 Henry III gave him the title, Prince of Wales.

But when Henry died, Llewelyn changed his mind. He did not attend Edward's coronation and refused to renew his homage to the new king, even when Edward took his entire court to Chester in 1275. The king was furious. He decided to force Llewelyn to obey him. So in the winter of 1277, he sent three separate armies into north Wales. They surrounded the Welsh, cut off their food supplies and forced them to surrender. Edward took away most of Llewelyn's land and much of his power, and he built royal castles at Rhuddlan, Flint, Aberystwyth and Builth to strengthen his position in Wales.

The Welsh did not give up without a struggle. In 1282 they rebelled again. This time Edward's armies crushed them completely and Llewelyn was killed. His head was cut off, sent to London and fixed on a spear on one of the gates of the Tower of London. It remained there for many years. The rest of his lands in Gwynedd were **confiscated** and Edward secured his hold by building three new castles at Harlech, Conway and Caernarvon. Welsh independence was at an end and English rule was established.

Still the Welsh had not finished. In 1294, they rose once more. This time they very nearly succeeded. But once supplies reached Edward's troops at Conway, the Welsh cause was hopeless. Edward took hundreds of hostages and imposed heavy fines. He also destroyed one of the local centres of rebellion, Llanfaes on Anglesey. It was there that he chose to build one last great fortress – Beaumaris.

Map of Wales and the border regions in the 1290s

Master James's masterpiece:
Beaumaris Castle

Beaumaris Castle, although never finished, is thought by many to be a perfect **concentric** castle. Like all Edward's other Welsh castles, it was built by Master James of St Georges. Edward had first come across his work in Savoy (now part of Switzerland) on his way back from the **crusades**. These castles were all built to impress and to stop the Welsh rebelling. They were the latest in castle technology, but they were also intended as royal homes.

SOURCE A

Barbican
The gates used to be the weakest part of a castle. Flanking towers make it almost impossible to break in through the gateway.

Round towers
Mining only works where square corners will collapse. Round towers also gave defenders a better view and field of fire.

Covering fire by defenders from higher inner walls
Defenders can concentrate their fire on the enemy from higher walls and remain almost totally safe inside the second wall.

Narrow outer bailey
This traps attackers and makes them an easy target for defenders to kill.

Deep-water harbour
Ships can sail right up to the castle and prevent a siege being effective.

Curtain walls
The first line of defence. The moat makes it hard to undermine them.

Beaumaris Castle

Finding out about castles

1 Compare Source A with the picture of Odiham Castle on page 70. How is Beaumaris different to Odiham Castle?

2 How might you attack Beaumaris Castle?

3 How might you defend Beaumaris Castle?

4 Do you think it would be easier to attack or defend Beaumaris Castle? Why?

5 Why do you think Beaumaris Castle was never completed?

6 Copy the diagram below. Add as many bullet points as you can to the Attack, and Defence boxes to show how castles changed from 1066 to 1295. A few bullet points have been done to help you get started.

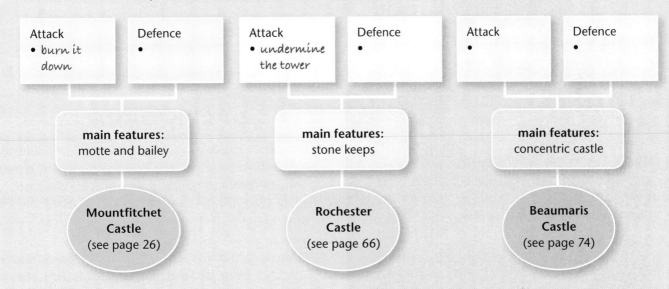

Attack	Defence
• burn it down	•

main features: motte and bailey

Mountfitchet Castle (see page 26)

Attack	Defence
• undermine the tower	•

main features: stone keeps

Rochester Castle (see page 66)

Attack	Defence
•	•

main features: concentric castle

Beaumaris Castle (see page 74)

Writing your brochure

Now you are going to produce a four-page guide to Beaumaris Castle. Your brochure should have four main sections:

Front cover. Include a title and a picture of Beaumaris Castle.

History of Beaumaris Castle. Use the information from 'In Defence of Honour' on page 72 to help you. Add pictures if you wish.

Design features of Beaumaris Castle. Explain why Beaumaris is the latest in castle design and how this is an improvement on earlier castles. Think about the work you did for Activity 6 above. Add pictures if you wish.

Beaumaris Castle as a place to live. Use the information from Life at Odiham Castle on page 68 to help you. Add pictures if you wish.

Think about these points when you are planning and writing the brochure:

- who will read your brochure
- the design of your brochure, including how much text and how many pictures there will be
- the language you will use and if you will need a glossary for special words
- use short active sentences
- include questions to keep readers interested
- use a mixture of past and present tenses
- include subheadings if you need to.

1290		1300		1307			
1290	1292	1295	1296	1297	1298	1305	1307
Queen Margaret of Scotland dies	Edward I nominates John Balliol as King of Scotland	Scottish rebellion	English army defeats King John Balliol – he is imprisoned in the Tower of London	Battle of Stirling Bridge	Battle of Falkirk	William Wallace is captured and executed	Edward I dies

William Wallace: the man behind the myth

SOURCE A

Mel Gibson as William Wallace in the film Braveheart

SOURCE B

Although the Scottish Lords owed their allegiance to the King of England, in their hearts they sympathised with Wallace. All of their followers joined Wallace's army and obeyed him as their leader and prince.

A version of an account by a contemporary chronicler

Over the centuries William Wallace has been many things to many people. He has been called an Outlaw, a Hero, a Freedom Fighter, a Traitor, the Guardian of Scotland, a Murderer, a **Martyr** and a **Patriot**. How can one man be all these things? What is the truth about William Wallace? How should we remember him?

The background

Edward I wanted to conquer Scotland. He had already defeated the Welsh. The death of Margaret, the three-year-old Queen of Scotland, gave him his chance in 1290. The Scottish nobles asked Edward to decide who should be their ruler. In 1292 he nominated John Balliol, but Edward made John pay homage to him as Overlord. This meant that Edward was able to control Scotland. He imprisoned many nobles, imposed heavy taxes on them and expected them to serve in his wars against France.

This angered the Scots and in 1295 King John rebelled. Edward's army marched North, defeated the Scots and in 1296 imprisoned their king in the Tower of London. The Scots were furious and the flames of rebellion spread. But who would lead them?

What do we know about William Wallace?

Very little evidence remains about William Wallace. It is not even certain when he was born. We do know he was the second son of a minor Scottish knight. He was educated, and was probably destined for a career in the Church. We first hear of Wallace in 1291 when he was declared an outlaw for killing an Englishman in Dundee. He seems to have been involved in a number of similar skirmishes before becoming famous for killing the English Sheriff of Lanark in May 1297. This was the month when, according to an English monk, 'The **perfidious** race of Scots began to rebel.' Wallace was just one of the leaders of the Scottish army that destroyed the English at the Battle of Stirling Bridge in September 1297.

After this success Wallace was knighted and appointed 'Guardian of Scotland'. As such, he was responsible for running the country and keeping Scotland independent. He now took the war into northern England and raided Newcastle. He fought Edward at the Battle of Falkirk in 1298, and lost. Little is known of the rest of his life until 1305 when he was betrayed and captured by the English. He was taken to London, tried and executed.

SOURCE C

William Wallace, a man ... hardened in cruelty, ... raging in madness ... was condemned to a most cruel but justly deserved death. He was drawn through the streets of London at the tails of horses, until he reached a gallows of unusual height, especially prepared for him; there he was suspended by a rope; but taken down while still alive, his bowels torn out and burned in a fire, his head then cut off, his body divided into four, and his quarters sent to four principal parts of Scotland.

Written by the chronicler, Matthew of Westminster

SOURCE D

Because he always stuck to his beliefs, Wallace is seen as a martyr. His refusal to settle for anything less than complete independence for Scotland is now seen as an inspiration. Wallace is famous for such a short time and there is little historical evidence for his actions. His importance is entirely down to his value to the Scottish people as a patriotic hero.

A modern historian

 ACTIVITY

You are going to write a paragraph explaining your view of William Wallace. To do this you need to think about why he has been remembered in different ways by different people. Look carefully at Sources A–E. For each source make a note of:

Which source?	Who wrote it or made it?	When was it written or made?	What other sources were available to the writer or maker?	What does it say about William Wallace?

Think about **why** each source gives a particular impression, good or bad, of Wallace. Now you should be able to write your paragraph.

SOURCE E

Window from Paisley Abbey, 1873, showing William Wallace as Samson. Samson appears in the Bible. He is a strong man, sent by God to fight the Philistines – the people from a more powerful neighbouring country. He finally dies a tragic death.

NEW WORDS

Allegiance
loyalty to a leader, a country or a belief

Martyr
a person who is killed or punished for their beliefs

Patriot
someone who loves their country and is willing to defend it

Perfidious
someone who cannot be trusted

1300
Population of London is about 80,000

1346
The Plague reaches Europe

1348
The Plague reaches England

1300 – 1348

What was it like living in a medieval town?

A fictional medieval town

> **Your challenge in this unit is to write a piece of historical fiction on what it was like to live in a medieval town. Writing good historical fiction is not easy. You need good ideas for the story and the skills to tell it well. You also need good research so that you can include realistic details. To help you, we are going to build up the story a piece at a time.**

Here is an extract from a book called *Matilda Bone* by Karen Cushman to give you an idea of how to start. Matilda is 14 years old and she is visiting a medieval town for the first time.

A gusty wind rattled shutters and set shop signs swinging as Matilda walked up the alley and turned onto Frog Road. She looked carefully about her, for she had arrived in near darkness and had not seen a town before. It was the first time she had been over a mile from the place where she was born. I never knew, she thought, there were so many people in the world, so many roads. And so many buildings, houses and shops crowded together, leaning **higgledy-piggledy** against each other. There were taverns and inns, dark and crowded and ominous. And churches with their bell towers pointing up to Heaven.

The streets grew more crowded. **Pedlars** called out, advertising their meagre winter wares. Onions and turnips, apples only slightly withered, salt meat, salt fish and salt! Church bells **clamoured** from every street corner. Beggars whined, dogs barked, pigs snorted as they rooted in the refuse. 'Have you any rats to kill?' cried one tradesman. 'Or clothes to mend?' called another as Matilda walked by.

She went through the Street of the Cupmakers past Shoemakers' Street, up along the river to Fish Street, and finally there was the market square.

The rain had stopped for a time; and the square was packed with people, bundled up in woollen scarves and gloves, buying and selling, begging and thieving.

Never before had Matilda been to a market. Her nose filled with the smell of beeswax candles, fine perfumes, onions and nutmeg. She pulled her cloak tighter against the wind as she paused to watch the magicians, acrobats and jugglers. She lingered at the silk stall and the leather booths, lost in the sights and sounds and smells, until her stomach rumbled a loud, hungry rumble. A chicken, she thought. It was not Lent, and she was not fasting today. Let us have a chicken, then, fat and juicy and golden from the fire.

She turned toward the Poultry, where chickens, lashed together by their feet, hung squawking and wriggling from the beams of the stalls. 'How much for a chicken?' she asked the poultryman.

'Three pennies.'

It was all she had. There would be no bread or cabbage. She thought again of the chicken, roasted golden.

'One chicken,' she said. 'Kindly kill it and pluck it clean.'

Finding out about towns

Think about what you have just read about Matilda Bone.

1 What makes the story about Matilda a good piece of fiction writing? To help you, consider the types of words the author uses.

   a) Find and write down five verbs (doing/action words) that create atmosphere and interest.

   b) Find and write down five adjectives (describing words that create atmosphere and interest.)

2 What could make the story about Matilda a useful piece of writing for learning about history? To help you, consider the information the author includes.

   a) Find and write down all the things on sale in the market.

   b) What do you notice about the names of the streets in the story?

The poultryman laughed. 'You bought it, you kill and pluck it,' he said, handing her a chicken by its feet. She reached out warily to grab it. The chicken squawked, Matilda squealed, and she dropped it as though it were on fire. The chicken made its escape amid baskets of duck feet and wild partridges.

'Where are my pennies?' asked the poultryman.

'Where is my chicken?' asked Matilda softly as she walked quickly away.

Fiction and history

Sometimes we can learn about history more easily by reading good historical fiction. It would be hard to find a history book or a medieval source that gave details about a person's feelings when they first visited a town.

In historical fiction an author can use **dialogue**. This can add interest, but also make some things easier to understand. Often historical fiction will contain **anachronisms**. These might be details of daily life or the way people speak. It doesn't mean that fiction is no use for learning about the past, but we have to be very careful what we call historical fact.

ACTIVITIES

Re-read the extract about Matilda and write down at least three examples that you think may be anachronisms.

NEW WORDS

Anachronism
something that didn't exist at that time, e.g. television

Clamoured
made a loud noise

Dialogue
speech

Higgledy-piggledy
all over the place

Pedlar
travelling seller of small items

Medieval towns: the 'big picture'

Towns grew steadily in size through most of the medieval period. London was by far the largest but still had a population of less than 100,000. Next in size came Bristol, York and Norwich. Smaller, but still important, were Exeter and Salisbury. All these towns were ports or centres for the wool industry.

Most towns had a population of a few hundred people. These market towns were closely linked to the surrounding villages. They held a weekly market and sometimes an annual fair. Ditches and wooden fences for defence sometimes surrounded towns. The larger and richer towns had stone walls and defended gateways.

Many people who went to live in towns were villagers who wanted more freedom. In the countryside, peasants were tied to the land and their lord by certain obligations. They had to work on the lord's land and couldn't sell their animals or marry off their daughters without getting his permission and paying him. In towns, people were not under these obligations. They might even help elect the mayor and other officials who ran the town.

 **ACTIVITIES**

Make a list of any major cities and towns you can think of in England today. There are now at least 15 with a population of over 250,000. Which ones are they? Are any of the big medieval towns shown in Source A also on your list?

SOURCE A

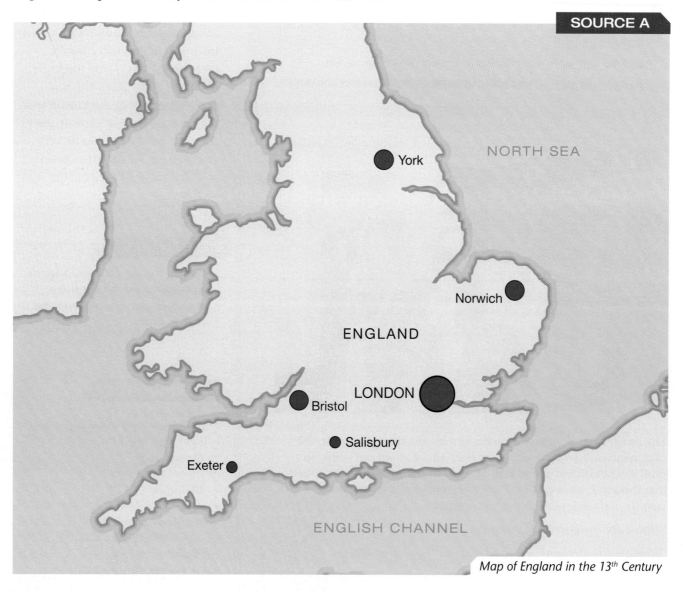

Map of England in the 13th Century

Bristol: a medieval town

Bristol was a port and even had a **mint** before the Normans invaded England in 1066. It grew up next to a crossing on the River Avon and the original name for Bristol meant 'the place of the bridge'.

The first settlement was on raised ground between the Rivers Avon and Frome. There were four main roads: Broad Street, High Street, Corn Street and Wine Street. The inner walls had four gates: St John's, St Nicholas' and St Leonard's Gate, and New Gate on the east of the town near the Norman castle. By 1400, many houses had been built outside the gates and new outer walls were built to protect the city.

SOURCE B

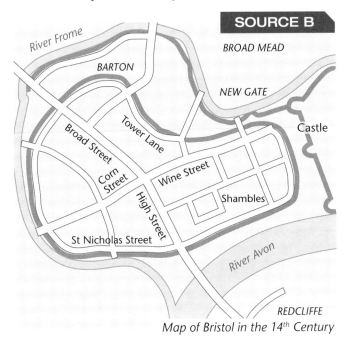

Map of Bristol in the 14th Century

SOURCE C

An illustration made in 1479 showing the four main streets and High Cross, Bristol

NEW WORDS

Mint
place where coins are made

ACTIVITIES

1. Study sources B and C. What trades do you think were carried out in Wine Street and Corn Street in medieval Bristol?

2. What is not accurate about Source C?

Finding out about towns

1. From what you have learnt or guessed so far, which of these adjectives could be used to describe life in a medieval town?

crowded	fun	hard	dirty	ordered
relaxed	quiet	clean	safe	noisy
dangerous	empty			

2. Write down any other adjectives you could use to describe medieval towns.

Medieval towns: the detail

Now read about some of the things that went on in medieval towns in more detail. As you read, remember that the descriptions are generalisations. Not every town had the same rules and things did change during the medieval period. A town might have had different laws in 1485 to those it had in 1066.

NEW WORDS

Cesspit
pit for sewage

Daub
mixture of clay and straw pushed into wattle

Wattle
fence of woven twigs

Bells

There were no clocks in ordinary peoples' homes in medieval times. Everyone lived within the sound of bells ringing at a local church. In towns, the bells told people when they should be doing things, for example:

4 or 5 am	Angelus bell	get up
6 am	Mass bell	shops and market open for townspeople
9 am	Mass bell	market opens for outsiders
12 am	Noon bell	lunchtime starts
5 or 6 pm	Evensong bell	most people stop work
8 or 9 pm	Curfew bell	town gates shut and everyone stays indoors

Merchants

Merchants were usually the richest people in a town. They controlled the trade of goods in and out of the town.

Craftsmen

Master craftsmen made things – anything from a pair of shoes to the wooden frame of a church roof. Craftsmen started learning their trade as apprentices, sometimes aged as young as seven. An apprentice lived and worked with a master craftsman for seven years. After this, he became a journeyman if his work was good enough. A journeyman was paid a wage and could travel around working for different master craftsmen. After several years, a journeyman could apply to become a master craftsman. Usually he had to make a 'masterpiece' as a test.

Craft guilds

Master craftsmen belonged to guilds. There were craft guilds for each type of work. Guilds were like clubs that looked after their members, but they also set rules about how work should be done. The guilds controlled how long craftsmen worked each day, the prices they charged and the quality of work. They also helped members who were ill and decided who could become master craftsmen.

Shops

Shops were small and open-fronted. They often sold only one type of product. Shops selling the same products were often together in the same street. This meant there could be a line of shops just selling bread or shoes, cloth or meat. Customers could easily compare quality and prices.

Houses

Town houses for shopkeepers, merchants and craftsmen were usually quite crowded. Many only had three rooms. There might be one room for the owner. The other rooms were used for cooking, working and for servants and apprentices to sleep in. Most houses had wooden frames. **Wattle** and **daub** was used to fill in the gaps between the timbers.

Money and food

In a medieval market most items only cost a few pennies. There were 12 (12d) pennies in a shilling (5p today) and twenty shillings in a pound. A builder in a town was paid about 6d a day. A knight was paid 2s a day. A small house cost just a few pounds to build. Look at the prices of some of the goods on sale in the market.

Eggs	5d a hundred
Sugar	1s 6d a pound
Raisins	3d a pound
Candles	1d a pound
Milk	1d a gallon
Beer	1d a gallon
Wine	10d a gallon
Sheep	2s each
Pigs	3s each

Animals and rubbish

Most people kept animals, often at least one pig. Sometimes the pigs were allowed to roam the streets searching for food. Food was easy to find as people usually threw their rubbish into the streets. There were no proper sewers, only open drains running down the streets. Few towns had public toilets and most homes had to rely on **cesspits**.

Finding out about towns

1 Re-read the descriptions of a medieval town on pages 82–83. Add adjectives to the list you made for the activity on page 81. Also make any changes to your list you think are necessary.

2 Now you are going to write the first part of your story about someone's first visit to a town. You must describe how they enter the town at one of its gates and walk through the streets to the market.

a) Imagine your character has lived all their life so far in a village (you could look at Unit 5 to help you). Decide on:

- whether to write in the first or third person
- whether your main character is a boy or a girl
- where your story is set. Will it be a town close to where you live? Or will you use the details about Bristol in this chapter to help you?
- whether the main character is shopping in the market or about to become an apprentice.

b) Your writing must contain good historical detail. You will need to include facts and vocabulary that clearly show the reader you are writing about life in a medieval town. Use the information in this unit to help you.

c) Do some research before you start writing if you need more information, for example about the town where you are setting your story or about apprentices.

d) Remember good fiction includes dialogue, lots of adjectives, strong verbs and repetition, and uses the five senses to create atmosphere. Jot down some ideas before you start writing.

e) Remember to check your punctuation and to start a new paragraph every time you change topic or someone speaks.

Here are a few examples of starter sentences, although you do not have to use them. You can probably think of something even better.

> Tom walked up to the town gates. He had never seen anything so big apart from his village church.

> I could smell the town even before I went through the gates.

> What struck Hugh most was the noise. He was used to the sounds of birds in the fields and woods. This was different!

Plague comes to town

We usually call the outbreak of plague in the medieval period the Black Death. It started in China and reached Europe in 1346. It reached London in 1348 and over the next two years spread north and west to affect the whole country. It has been estimated that perhaps 25 million people in Europe died, three-quarters of the inhabitants in some areas.

The outbreak became known as the Black Death because of the black swellings and dark blotches that appeared on victims' bodies. A person first knew they had the disease when a swelling appeared in the groin or armpit. They could be dead within 24 hours but would usually live for two or three days. During that time they might show a range of **symptoms**. They might have **convulsions**, high temperature, vomiting, splitting headaches, red eyes, sleeplessness and swollen tongues covered in fur.

Plague victims from a later 16th Century source

ACTIVITIES

Make a note of any symptoms of the plague you might use in the next part of your story.

What caused the plague

Many people believed that God had sent the plague as a punishment. Some thought the plague was linked to bad smells. In some towns, orders were given to clean up the rubbish, but this failed to stop the plague spreading. People fled when the plague reached their town or village and this often just helped to spread the disease. Many tried prayer or **pilgrimage** to a holy place. In several countries, groups of people called flagellants marched from town to town. As they travelled, they prayed and beat themselves with whips, asking for God's forgiveness.

In fact, people then had no idea what really caused the plague. Today we know the disease was spread by the fleas on black rats. When the rats died, the fleas bit people and animals, passing on the disease. Sometimes the disease spread when there weren't any rats – the fleas survived in clothing or trade goods, ready to infect towns or villages.

Flagellants on the march, 1349

Physician
  trained doctor
Pilgrimage
  religious journey to a holy place

Finding out about towns

Add a second section to your story about how plague comes to the town and how people react. Use the following advice to help you.

a) Make a note of any symptoms of the plague you could use.

b) Plan how your main character will react, for example to rumours in the market about the plague.

c) Decide on some new characters to introduce, for example victims, a **physician** or a priest. You could have a band of flagellants marching into the town. You could include dialogue to show the townspeoples' reactions to men whipping themselves in the streets.

d) Do some research if you need more detailed information to make your story realistic, for example about medical treatments.

ACTIVITIES

1 Write two sentences about what people at the time thought spread the plague.

2 Write two sentences about what we know today about the spread of the plague.

EXTENSION ACTIVITY

If you have time, add a final section to your story about how the disease takes hold of the town. Describe how many people begin to fall sick and die. What does the main character do – try to help, join the flagellants, flee back to the village or notice a swelling in their armpit or groin? You could look at Case Study 3 on pages 88–89 for more ideas.

The effects of the **Black Death**

Henry Knighton was a priest who lived through the plague years. He wrote a chronicle that described the spread of the plague and what happened afterwards. It is one of the best pieces of evidence we have about the Black Death in England. All the extracts here are from Henry's chronicle.

SOURCE A

Many buildings large and small, in all cities, towns and villages, had collapsed, and completely fallen to the ground for lack of inhabitants.

SOURCE B

If anyone wanted to employ labourers, he had to pay them what they asked – or lose his fruit and crops.

SOURCE C

Before the plague, a priest would live in a village and take all the services for £3 a year – but now no none will do the job unless they are paid £20 a year.

SOURCE D

Everything became so dear that anything that in the past had been worth a penny, was now worth four or five pence. And all foodstuffs became exceedingly dear.

SOURCE E

The king ordered that labourers should not be paid more than they usually received. The labourers were so proud and hostile that they took no notice of the king's law.

SOURCE F

There was a great lack of servants to do anything.

SOURCE G

There was such a great shortage of priests everywhere that many churches were abandoned. None of the normal services were held.

SOURCE H

Many small villages were completely deserted. All those who had lived in them were dead.

SOURCE I

Lords either had to let the serfs off the services, or else accept money instead. Unless they did this the serfs ran away and left their houses and the land to go to ruin.

SOURCE J

Shortly after the plague a large number of men whose wives had died became priests, although many of them could not even write. They could read a little, but did not understand what they were reading.

1. Make a copy of this table and write the letter for each extract from the chronicle under the correct heading. You can put the letter for an extract under more than one heading.

Lack of people	The Church	Prices	Wages

2. Which effects of the plague do you think rich people thought were most important? Explain your answer in a few sentences.

3. Which effects of the plague do you think poor people thought were most important? Explain your answer in a few sentences.

Monks with plague being blessed by a priest

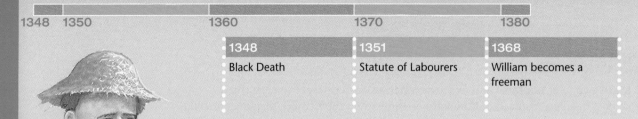
1348 – 1381

What was it like living in the countryside?

A gruesome tale

On Friday, 14 June 1381, a crazed mob made its way to the Tower of London. It burst in by force and dragged out the Archbishop of Canterbury, Sir Simon Sudbury, the King's Treasurer, Robert Hales and some other ministers. At Tower Hill the mob beheaded them. It took eight blows to hack off the archbishop's head. His **mitre** was then nailed back onto his skull, before the heads were placed on lances and carried through the city to London Bridge, where they were fixed on stakes for all to see.

Many others were beheaded that night. In one place there was a heap of about 40 headless bodies. There were dead bodies in virtually every street and many houses were destroyed. Why did this happen?

It began in Brentwood, Essex on 31 May and quickly spread across the country. Men cleaned swords and longbows, sharpened axes and knives and took down scythes and sickles. In Kent rebels attacked Dartford, captured Rochester Castle and went on to Maidstone. There they freed John Ball from prison and made Wat Tyler their leader. Then they headed for London, destroying manor houses and legal documents, and gathering men as they went.

By the evening of Wednesday, 12 June, 60,000 men were camped outside London. The men of Essex, with supporters from Hertfordshire, Suffolk and Cambridgeshire, were in the fields of Mile End. The men of Kent were at Blackheath, 8 kilometres from the city. Richard II and his advisers, not knowing what to do, retreated to the Tower of London.

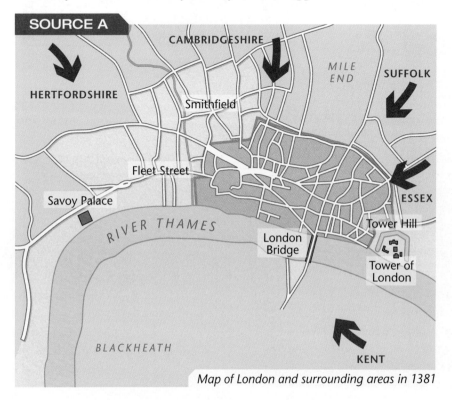

SOURCE A

Map of London and surrounding areas in 1381

NEW WORDS

Mitre
archbishop's hat and sign of his position

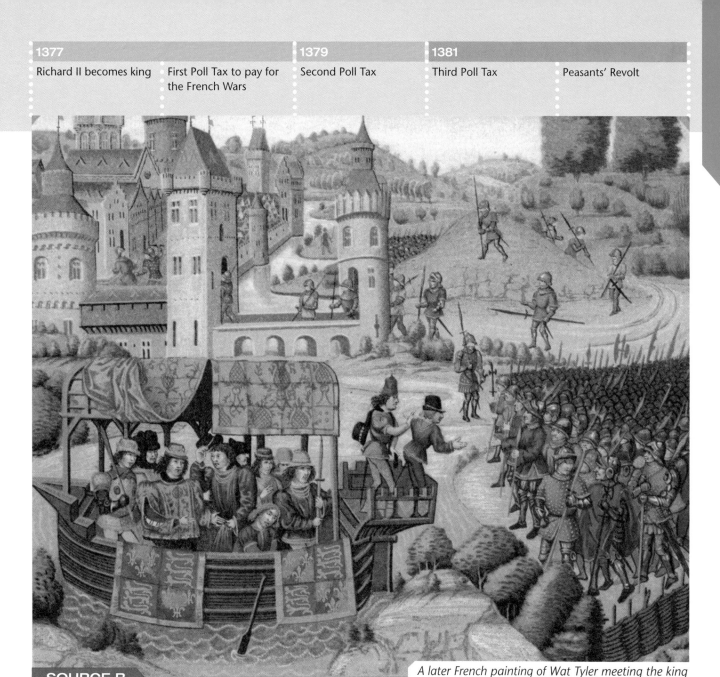

SOURCE B

A later French painting of Wat Tyler meeting the king

The next day King Richard and his advisers were rowed down the Thames towards Blackheath to speak with the rebels. They were met by a chorus of jeers and insults. So, on the insistence of Richard's ministers, the royal barge moved slowly back towards the Tower.

This persuaded the rebels to enter the city. The people of London opened the gates and welcomed them in. Men from Kent and the surrounding area poured across London Bridge, while the men from Essex marched in through Aldgate. They broke open the prison in Fleet Street and burned Savoy Palace, the magnificent home of the king's uncle, the Duke of Lancaster, John of Gaunt to the ground.

From his refuge in the Tower, 14-year-old Richard watched flames light up the night sky as thousands of drunken rebels rampaged through London, burning and murdering.

Early the next morning, King Richard left the Tower, escorted by many nobles and knights, and rode to Mile End. There he met the rebels and granted all their demands. He promised that all 'traitors' to the people would be executed. He then told them to go home. Although many did, many more remained. They wanted the blood of the traitors. They took the law into their own hands and many were killed that day.

On 15 June Richard met the remaining rebels at Smithfield. He was accompanied by some of his **courtiers** and William Walworth, the Lord Mayor of London. Wat Tyler rode forward on a pony. He dismounted, shook the king's hand roughly and spoke to him rudely and aggressively. Tossing a dagger from hand to hand, he made further demands of the king and swore that he would not leave until they were met. The king agreed and ordered the rebels to disperse.

It was a hot day and Tyler sent for a jug of water. He rinsed his mouth and spat the water out. Then he climbed back onto his pony. One of the king's men shouted at Tyler for his rudeness to the king.

Tyler tried to stab him with his dagger, but William Walworth stopped him. Tyler grew very angry and stabbed the mayor. But Walworth wore armour and was not harmed. He drew his own dagger and struck back at Tyler, giving him a deep cut in the neck and a great blow on his head. Another of the king's men ran his sword through the body two or three times and Wat Tyler died.

Then Richard II bravely rode up to the rebels. They wanted revenge for their leader's death and were preparing for battle. Calmly he asked them what was wrong and told them he was their king and they should follow him. And the Peasants' Revolt ended and the rebels went home.

SOURCE C

A later French painting of Wat Tyler being killed

However, once the mob had been safely dispersed, the king broke all his promises. His soldiers arrested any rebels left in London. Everyone in the city had to swear loyalty to the king on a Bible. Royal forces went into the countryside, rooting out the ringleaders and crushing any resistance. John Ball was captured and hanged, drawn and quartered on 15 July. Roadside gallows became a common sight. Soon they creaked under the weight of rotting bodies. The king was once again in control.

NEW WORDS

Courtier
adviser to the king

ACTIVITIES

1. How did King Richard deal with the rebels? Copy and complete the table below to help you organise your ideas.

Action	Your view on the king's action	Why do you think this?
Retreating to the Tower	(Was it a sensible or cowardly action?)	(Because reinforcements were needed or to encourage the rebels?)
Rowing down the river to meet the rebels		
Meeting the rebels at Mile End		
Meeting with Wat Tyler at Smithfield		
Breaking his promises after the revolt		

2. Use your answers to Activity 1 to decide which of the following statements you agree with. You might agree with more than one.
   - King Richard dealt very well with the rebels.
   - King Richard dealt badly with the rebels.
   - King Richard did the best he could in the circumstances.
   - King Richard was badly advised by his ministers.
   - King Richard acted bravely.
   - King Richard betrayed the rebels.

3. Write a paragraph to explain your views about how King Richard acted.

Finding out about the Peasants' Revolt

1. In this unit you are going to write an essay about the causes of the Peasants' Revolt. Look back over the story. Are there any clues in it that suggest why the revolt might have happened?

1385:
A peasant remembers

'My name is William and I'm going to tell you a bit about my life.'

'I live in Long Sutton, a village in Lincolnshire. You can see where it is in Source A. I'm a **freeman** now, but I haven't always been. Until 1368 I was a **villein**. I suppose I'm lucky. I'm 50 years old, so I've had a long life. I've seen lots of changes, some good and some bad. I survived the Black Death, but watched several of my family and many friends die. I've seen my wages increase and my standard of living improve, until the king passed a law stopping all that. A few years ago I heard John Ball **preach** and was impressed by what he said. I've struggled to pay the **Poll Tax**. And since the Peasants' Revolt four years ago, I've listened to tales of the king's broken promises and bodies being left to rot on roadside gallows.'

'But despite all of the changes, in some ways life is the same as it always was. Let me tell you a bit about things in a bit more detail.'

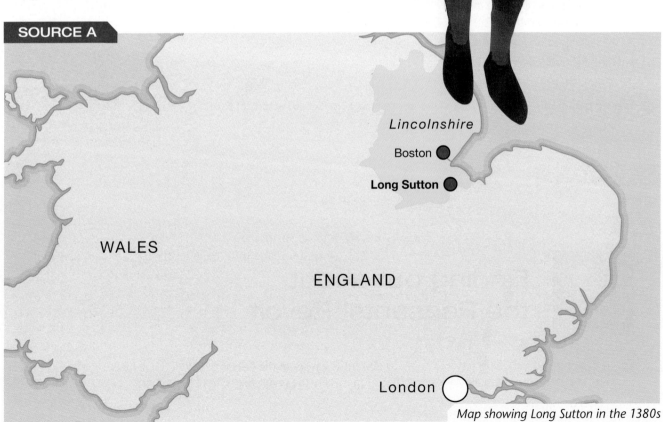

SOURCE A

Lincolnshire

Boston ●

Long Sutton ●

WALES

ENGLAND

London ○

Map showing Long Sutton in the 1380s

Living

'This is where we live. It's not as crowded as it used to be when the children were at home. They've all married now and have children of their own – at least the ones that have survived.'

'I built the cottage myself with timber, wattle and daub, but I needed a bit of help with the roof from the **thatcher**. We put in some windows a few years ago. Glass is so expensive! The floor is beaten earth. There's an open fire on a stone slab in the middle. It can get very smoky and it's also quite dark. **Rushlights** give us some light, but they're not very bright and in winter we often go to bed soon after sunset.'

An artist's interpretation of a peasants cottage in summer

NEW WORDS

Freeman
person who rents land from a lord

Poll tax
a tax paid by all adults

Preach
give a religious talk

Rushlight
reeds dipped in mutton fat

Thatcher
person who makes roofs from straw

Vat
a large container for storing liquid

Villein
person who worked unpaid for the lord in return for a small plot of land

'We've got quite a bit of furniture – a table, three benches, a chair and a mattress. The carpenter made most of these for us. We've got a basin and jug, three large brass pots and two brass pans, two straw baskets, four linen sheets, two tablecloths, two towels, a mortar and pestle, knives and wooden ladles, bowls, mugs and spoons. We also own three wooden barrels, four **vats** and two tubs. When my wife isn't working on the land, she earns some extra money for us by spinning wool from our sheep. We're better off than we were!'

An artist's interpretation of a peasants cottage in winter

'In winter we share our cottage with some of our animals. There are the oxen. We can't plough without them! Then there are the cows and calves, pigs, sheep, geese and hens. I even managed to buy a mare three years ago. And I own my own plough!'

'We eat well enough most of the year, although supplies do get rather low by late spring or early summer. I'm sure you've spotted the pig hanging from the rafters. We don't have enough fodder to feed all the animals through the winter, so in autumn we **slaughter** most of them and smoke or salt the meat to **preserve** it. We grow as much fruit and vegetables as we can in our toft. We have apple, pear and plum trees, and cabbages, carrots, onions and leeks. We even use the nettles, dandelions and ground elder! Can you see our beehive in the corner?

Of course, we also have wheat, oats, beans, peas and barley on our land in the three big open fields. Most of the barley is used for brewing ale – it's safer to drink than the water! I suppose we're quite lucky that the forest and marsh land around the village does not belong to the king, so we sometimes eat venison and fowl when we can catch them and there is plenty of fish in the rivers and rabbits in the fields.'

Women catching rabbits with a net and a ferret

ACTIVITIES

1. Why do you think the cottage got so smoky?

2. Why did lots of peasant cottages burn down?

3. What do you think the wooden barrels, vats and tubs were used for?

4. What was kept upstairs?

5. Why do you think food was sometimes in very short supply in late spring and early summer?

6. Use what you have learnt so far to draw up a menu of what William might have eaten for a week.

NEW WORDS

Preserve
    prepare food for storage
Slaughter
    kill

Working

'Most of my time is spent working in the fields. I have 30 acres, 10 acres in each of the three fields. On a good day the oxen and I can plough an acre, but more often it is less, especially if I have to take the plough to the blacksmith to be repaired. I need to use my neighbour's oxen – I have two, but you need more to pull a plough.'

'In October and November we plough, **harrow** and sow the wheat field. That is also when we slaughter most of our animals and then salt them. In the hard winter weather, we **thresh** the wheat or barley, getting it ready for sale or for the mill. We get the carpenter to mend any broken tools in winter too. In February and March we plough, harrow and sow the barley or oats field. In spring we let the animals onto the **fallow** field – they provide manure to make the land more fertile. In May we cut the hay – a good hay crop means at least some of our animals will survive the winter. We also have to shear all the sheep then.'

'August and September is harvest time. The long days are taken up with cutting the corn with a sickle – very hard work! Everyone in the village has to turn out and help – either in cutting, stacking or carting the wheat or barley back to the barns. Our well-being for the whole year depends on how good the harvest is – if we get eight bushels per acre, it is an excellent harvest. We all pray for fine weather at harvest time!'

'Of course, all the normal jobs have to carry on every day – looking after the animals, milking the cows and sheep, making butter and cheese, tending the crops in our garden, brewing ale, fetching water, collecting the eggs and taking grain to the miller, so we have flour for bread.'

Sheep in a wattle pen

'It's a good job there's plenty of common or waste land and woods around the village – they provide grazing for the flocks of village animals and timber for building, firewood and fencing. If all goes well, we just about make enough to pay our **tithe** to the Church and rent to the lord. We need to have some money to buy the things we can't grow and to pay our taxes. Thank goodness for sheep! Their fleeces are in great demand in Boston, for export to Calais. It's still a real struggle some years, but at least we're a lot better off than those poor **cottagers** who live in the huts on the waste land. I don't know how they survive.'

NEW WORDS

Cottager
person who had no land or rights

Fallow
field left unsown

Harrow
break down the soil after ploughing

Thresh
remove the grains from the straw

Tithe
a tax of 10% of income paid by everyone to the Church

ACTIVITIES

1. Which times of the year were the busiest for peasants?

2. At which times of the year was there less to do?

3. Look carefully at Source C. Use the text above to write a caption for the picture.

4. Make a list of words or phrases from the text that tell us that William is better off than he used to be.

5. Make a list of words or phrases from the text that tell us that William still has a very hard life.

6. Do you think people at the time would have considered William to be well off? Explain your answer.

Looking **back**

'Things are better now than they used to be. When I was a boy, back in the 1340s, we had to work for the lord three days a week for nothing. In return we got some land of our own in the fields to grow our food. We had to pay 'fines' to the lord at Easter and Christmas, and ask for permission to get married or leave the village. That was expensive and it was a very hard life – but then things slowly started to improve.'

Why was there a revolt in 1381?

1348: the Black Death

'The Black Death had a devastating effect on my village. I was only 13 years old at the time, but I remember it well. Over half of the people in the village died – whole families wiped out! Even the priest! We had to bury people in a mass grave, outside the churchyard, and without a priest to pray for them! We couldn't get all the harvest in or look after all the animals. The lord didn't get much rent that year, I can tell you. I was lucky – I survived, even when the **Pestilence** came back twice more.'

SOURCE A

A mass grave

'But some good did come from the Black Death. There was a real shortage of labour. The lord found it hard to get **tenants** so I was able to rent some land. Wages went up too. For once we had some power over the nobles and we used it to become a little better off. If they didn't pay higher wages or do away with fines, men just ran away to work in other parts of the country.'

'The king and the rich tried to stop it, of course. They passed the Statute of Labourers in 1351. This law said that wages should be no more than they were before the Black Death, but everyone, including the lords, ignored it. A few peasants were put in prison for demanding higher wages, but most lords were so desperate for workers that they just paid the going rate. You could get as much land as you wanted, and more. There was plenty of land turned over to sheep, because there were no villeins to work it.'

NEW WORDS

Pestilence
the plague, Black Death
Tenant
person who rents land from a lord

 ACTIVITIES

1. Do you think William was better or worse off as a result of the Black Death?

2. Do you think peasants were better off or worse off after the Black Death?

3. Why didn't the Statute of Labourers of 1351 work?

1368: freedom and taxes

'Our lord is John O'Gaunt, the mighty Duke of Lancaster, the king's uncle. In 1368, he decided the only thing to do was to rent out the whole manor to us – tenants, villeins, cottagers and all. At a great meeting in the church we agreed to pay him a fixed rent of £128. 13sh. 6d each year for the whole 1,000 acres. That way he had a guaranteed income, but we got to manage our own affairs and decide for ourselves who had what land. It was a lot of money, but we paid it and made some money for ourselves as well. No more fines or unpaid labour! That's when I put the first glass in my windows ... the same sort of thing was happening right across the country.'

Poll tax

'The problems began when Richard II became king in 1377. There are always problems when you have a young king and Richard was just ten. All the nobles were trying to run the country and no one was really in control. And then there were the wars with France. He kept losing. But *we* had to pay for them. A poll tax! Is that fair? Charging everyone the same whether they are rich or poor? In 1377 it was 4d for every man and woman over 16. In 1379 it was another 4d, but at least this time the rich had to pay more – an earl paid £4, a mayor of a large town, £2.'

'It was about this time I heard John Ball preach. He had been a priest, but was thrown out of his church because of his views. He wandered from place to place, preaching in the open air. He argued that if everyone had to pay the same taxes, then they should have a vote in Parliament and a say in running the country. He said no one should have to do unpaid labour for their lord and everyone should be equal. They quickly put him in prison, but that didn't stop us talking! What ideas! Me, the same as John O'Gaunt or the king!'

'Then in 1381 there was another poll tax and this time it was 12d for every man and woman over 15. That's a lot of money to find all at once. No wonder people were upset. Lots of people just refused to pay and that's when the trouble started. Enough was enough! In some places, tax collectors were murdered. Wat Tyler led the Kent peasants to London to ask the young king to stop listening to his bad advisers and to free all villeins. They freed John Ball and he joined them. So did the men from Essex and elsewhere. It was quite a protest. But you already know the rest of the story.'

EXTENSION ACTIVITY

John Ball argued that everyone is equal and he was put in prison! Do you agree or disagree with him?

Finding out about the Peasants' Revolt

1 In this unit you have found out about the causes of the Peasants' Revolt. Here is a list of the main ones:
   a) Richard II was badly advised
   b) the preaching of John Ball
   c) defeat in the French Wars
   d) the Black Death
   e) poll taxes
   f) Statute of Labourers
   g) Wat Tyler's leadership of the peasants
   h) unfree peasants
   i) the king was very young.

   Using the information in the unit, explain briefly why each of the points listed above was one of the causes of the revolt.

2 Decide which causes you think were long term and which were short term. (Long term causes set the scene and begin the process. Short term causes are much more immediate and trigger the event.)

3 Sort the causes into an order of importance. Put the one you think is the most important at the top of your list, down to the least important at the bottom.

4 Compare your list with a partner's. Discuss the differences and then make changes to the order if you wish.

5 Now you are going to write an essay entitled 'Why was there a peasants' revolt in 1381?' Use your answers to the activities in this unit as a framework for organising the information.

The **100 Years'** War

The 100 Years' War was not really a continuous war that lasted for 100 years. It was a series of battles and **campaigns** that English kings fought to try and gain, or keep, land in France. At first the English were often able to defeat bigger French armies by using archers armed with longbows. They could shoot arrows with enough power to get through the armour of the French knights. However, in the end, it was the French that won the war and the city of Calais was the only place left in English hands.

English successes

1340 Battle of Sluys
The English fleet destroyed the French forces in a naval battle and stopped them invading England.

1346 Battle of Crécy
English longbow men helped win a decisive victory against a larger French army.

1347 Calais
After a year-long siege, the English captured Calais.

1356 Battle of Poitiers
The English captured the French king and about 2,000 of his men.

1364 Battle of Auray
The French leader was captured.

1367 Battle of Navarrette
24,000 English defeated 60,000 French and Spaniards.

1387 Battle of Margate
The English captured or destroyed 100 enemy ships.

1327–1377
EDWARD III

The Black Death arrives in England.

1377–1399
RICHARD II

The Peasants' Revolt

French successes

SOURCE B

1380 Chateauneuf-de-Randon
After a hard siege, the French captured the city but their leader, Du Guesclin, died.

Joan of Arc saves the town of Orleans

ACTIVITIES

1. Did the French or the English have most successes?

2. Which side had the biggest successes?

3. Suggest three reasons why the English lost in the end.

The Battle of Crécy

NEW WORDS

- **Campaign**
  series of battles

1415 Battle of Verneuil
English archers killed about half of a French and Scots army.

1415 Battle of Agincourt
An army of 6,000 Englishmen defeated a French force of 20,000.

1431
Joan of Arc was burned at the stake at Rouen.

The Wars of the Roses start in England

1399–1413	1413–1422	1422–1461
HENRY IV	HENRY V	HENRY VI

1421 Battle of Beauge
French and Scottish forces defeated the English in Normandy.

1429 Orleans
Joan of Arc saved the town from an English siege.

1449 Rouen
The people of Rouen revolted against the English, who surrendered the city.

1453 Battle of Castillon
English forces attacked the French besieging the town but were heavily defeated.

1429 Jargeau
Joan of Arc captured the fortress near Orleans.

1450 Battle of Formigny
The French used cannon to help destroy an English army that had retreated into the town.

1429 Battle of Patay
Joan of Arc's army killed more than 2,000 English soldiers.

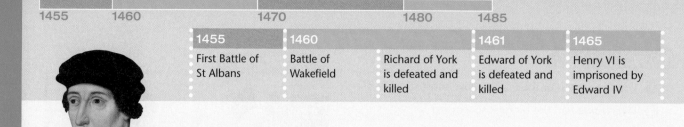

1455	1460		1461	1465
First Battle of St Albans	Battle of Wakefield	Richard of York is defeated and killed	Edward of York is defeated and killed	Henry VI is imprisoned by Edward IV

1455 – 1485

Wars of the Roses: who will be king?

The first battle at St Albans

SOURCE A

A painting of the meeting between the Duke of York and the Earl of Warwick

King Henry VI reached St Albans at 9am on 22 May 1455. He had 2,000 men with him, but he walked straight into a trap. The Duke of York, the Earl of Warwick and 3,000 men were waiting in Key Field, southeast of St Peter's Street. When the king and his men marched into St Peter's Street, the duke's men barred the street at both ends. The duke demanded that King Henry hand over the Duke of Somerset, 'a man disloyal to his country who reduced England to a state of misery.' The king told the Yorkists to leave or 'I shall destroy them, every mother's son and they shall be hanged, drawn and quartered.'

The royal troops prepared to defend the town centre. They erected **barricades** across St Peter's Street. The king set up his banner in the street, halfway between the abbey and the parish church, opposite the Castle Inn.

The Yorkists attacked the barricades, but were beaten back. Then the Earl of Warwick and 600 men burst into Holywell Street, which led into St Peter's Street. They broke in opposite the abbey gatehouse through the back gardens between two inns, The Cross Keys and The Chequer. As they attacked, the Earl's men blew trumpets and shouted, 'A Warwick! A Warwick! A Warwick!' Then York's troops broke into St Peter's Street at the opposite end. Both sides fought savagely.

The aged Abbot of St Albans was watching and was horrified by what he saw. He later recalled, 'I saw a man fall with his brains beaten out, another with a broken arm, a third with his throat cut and a fourth with a stab wound in his chest, while the whole street was strewn with corpses.'

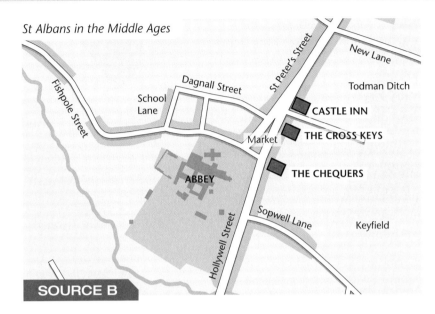

St Albans in the Middle Ages

SOURCE B

The king was wounded by an arrow in the neck and he took refuge in a **tanner's** cottage. The royal banner was left standing against a wall. The king's men either fled into the surrounding fields or else begged for mercy.

The Duke of Somerset, who had once had a dream that he would die under a castle, retreated inside the Castle Inn. When the Yorkists began to batter the doors, he came out fighting. He killed four of his opponents before being cut down beneath the inn sign of a castle. The whole battle lasted just half an hour.

Adapted from The Wars of the Roses *by Desmond Seward*

ACTIVITIES

1. What do you think happened next in the story? Choose one of these possible answers OR write your own.

   - King Henry was good to his word. The Duke of York was arrested and executed.

   - King Henry died because of his neck wound. The next day the Duke of York was made King.

   - The Duke of York knelt before the wounded King Henry. He swore he never meant to harm the king. Henry forgave him.

   - The Duke of York captured King Henry and murdered him. Then he marched to London.

NEW WORDS

Barricade
a barrier to stop the movement of a crowd or army

Tanner
a craftsman who works with leather

What happened after the battle?

When the fighting was over, the Duke of York went to see King Henry. He knelt by the wounded king's bed and said he did not want to harm him. Henry forgave him. The next day they rode together into London, where Henry's wife, Margaret of Anjou and his two-year-old son, Edward had taken refuge in the Tower of London.

Perhaps fewer than 100 men died in the Battle of St Albans, so why was it important?

The battle was the first of a dozen major battles in what has become known as the Wars of the Roses. The fighting was spread over 30 years. During the wars, one king died on the battlefield and one was murdered. Scores of captured knights and nobles were beheaded. The fighting did not affect ordinary people very much, but the lives of those with a title were at risk.

The struggle was to decide which part of the royal family would run the country. Both were directly descended from Edward III, but one part was called the House of York and the other, the House of Lancaster.

Finding out about the Wars of the Roses

In this unit you are going to write the script for a short, factual TV programme about the Wars of the Roses. To make your programme you will need:
- a title
- a script
- a storyboard.

You will get help in writing your script over the next few pages. In the script for the narrator of your programme you must explain:
- why the fighting started
- about soldiers and war
- who was involved
- how we know what we know
- about women in the Wars of the Roses.

1 Think of a working title for your programme. A working title is one that you can change right up to the time you finish your final script.

Making a television programme is not just about writing a script. You also need to think about what the viewers will see on screen. Filmmakers plan this by making a storyboard, which is a series of simple sketches showing the start of each new scene. There are also notes about camera views and actions.

2 Here is a simple storyboard for a film about the Battle of St Albans. Read the captions and notice the language used for the camera shots. Which caption would the director use for each sketch on the storyboard?

a) *Close-up shot* of King Henry wounded by an arrow.
b) *High camera angle* view of Warwick's men breaking into Holywell Street.
c) *Long shot and zoom* to horrified abbot watching street fighting.
d) *High camera angle* of King Henry's men marching into St Albans.
e) *Fade out* Duke of Somerset dead outside the Castle Inn.
f) *Pan* of Henry's men as they find their route blocked.
g) *Zoom* shot of fighting at the barricades in St Peter's Street.

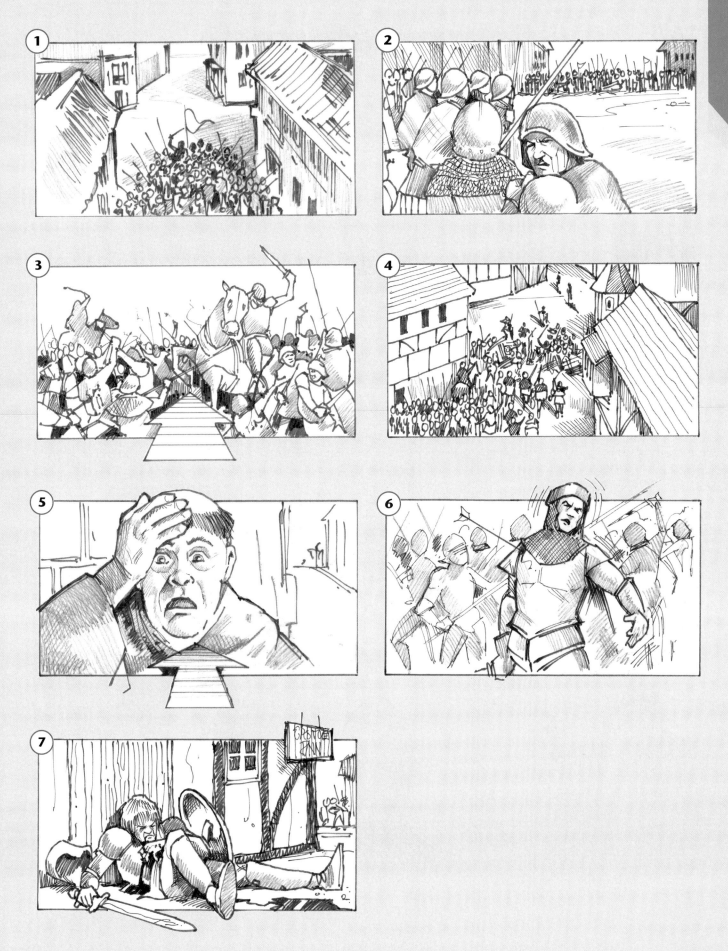

Why the **fighting started**

The story of the Wars of Roses started long before the Battle of St Albans. In 1399, Henry Bolingbroke forced his cousin Richard II off the throne. Henry became Henry IV. He was a strong leader and it looked as if his family, the House of Lancaster, would continue to rule from then on. But Henry's grandson, Henry VI, was a weak king. He appointed unpopular nobles to advise him.

In 1453 Henry became ill. Henry's cousin, Richard Duke of York was named Protector of England. He ruled for ten months until the king recovered. York had been Henry's heir to the throne, but when Henry got better, York gathered an army and marched on St Albans.

Finding out about The Wars of the Roses

Explaining why the fighting started is probably the most complicated part of your programme. You can use the paragraphs above as your script for this section. How can you make this story easier for the viewers of your programme to understand? One way would be to choose the right pictures to show on screen.

1. Choose three of these pictures to use and be ready to explain your choices.

2. Remind yourself of the storyboard captions for the Battle of St Albans. Now write a storyboard caption for each of the pictures you have chosen here.

1

2

3

4

5

6

Soldiers and **war**

York and Henry settled their argument after the battle, but soon Henry became ill again. Once more Richard Duke of York was made Protector of England until Henry got better a few months later. Trouble continued to brew between the House of York and the House of Lancaster. Finally in 1459 this led to the Battle of Blore Heath. Here the Lancastrians were defeated.

Finding out about The Wars of the Roses

1 This is the storyboard for the next section in your TV programme. Study it carefully and then read sources A–F on pages 110 to 111. These give you information on the battles of the Wars of the Roses and the soldiers who fought in them.

Front view of the army ready for battle
Pan across front of army picking out archers, knights and foot soldiers

Bodies lying in a deep river valley
Zoom down on massed bodies

Modern reconstruction of the Battle of Towton
High camera angle of armies just before the battle starts

Archers firing bows
Level camera angle

Battle of Towton
1461
York

Name of battle, date and result
Dissolve for next battle detail

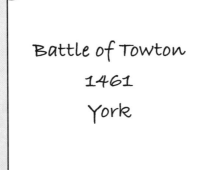

Knight ready for battle
Close-up shot

Finding out about the Wars of the Roses

1 Study the information in Sources A–F. Add details about battles, armour and weapons to your notes.

Battles	Date	Winner
Blore Heath	1459	York
Northampton	1460	York
Towton	1461	York
Barnet	1471	York
Tewkesbury	1471	York
Bosworth	1485	Lancaster

The main battles of the Wars of the Roses

SOURCE B

Most ordinary soldiers carried pole arms

SOURCE C

Only knights and nobles could afford to fight in armour like this

SOURCE D

Archers	Most battles started with a battle between the archers. A good archer could keep six arrows in the air at once. Some arrows could punch through armour. No one was safe until the archers ran out of arrows.
Armour	Armour was very expensive. Many ordinary soldiers wore an open-faced helmet called a sallet. They sometimes wore a brigadine. This was a jacket with small steel plates stitched inside the cloth. Leg armour was not often used as most men fought on foot.
Pole arms	Most ordinary foot soldiers were armed with a bill. This was usually over 2 metres long. It had a spike, a cutting blade and sometimes a hook. It could be used to stab, slash and pull men from their horses.
Guns	Simple handguns and cannon were used in several battles. They were not very reliable, but their noise and smoke must have been frightening.

Information on archers and weapons

Both sides had large numbers of well-trained archers in their armies

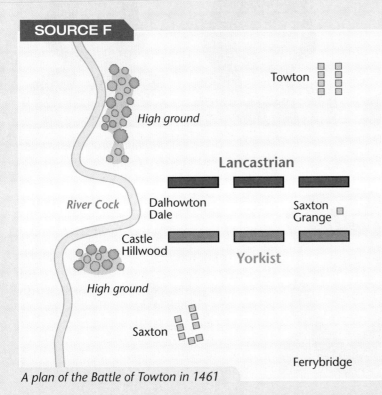

Towton

High ground

Lancastrian

River Cock
Dalhowton Dale

Saxton Grange

Castle Hillwood

Yorkist

High ground

Saxton

Ferrybridge

A plan of the Battle of Towton in 1461

Towton was probably the largest battle fought in medieval England. As many as 28,000 men were killed or wounded. The battle began in a snowstorm. The wind was against the Lancastrians and their arrows fell short of the enemy. Hand-to-hand fighting went on for hours. At last the Lancastrians began to flee. Thousands of them were killed, or drowned, trying to escape across the River Cock.

The Battle of Towton in 1461

2 Now write the final version of your script for the story of the Battle of Towton. Remember to look back at the storyboard pictures on page 109. You can also mention some of the other battles in the Wars of the Roses.

EXTENSION ACTIVITY

1 Find the names, dates and winner of other battles during the Wars of the Roses.

2 Compare the armour in Source C with that worn by knights at the Battle of Hastings in 1066.

3 Find out how early cannon worked.

4 Find out what materials were used to make medieval bows and arrows.

Who was **involved**?

Researching the Wars of the Roses is a bit like reading a medieval telephone directory. There are so many, often similar, names. It can get very confusing! You will need some detail about a few of these people in your programme, but you will need to present it in a way that will not confuse your audience.

Finding out about
The Wars of the Roses

1 Study this possible storyboard for introducing the most important people in the story.

Henry VI

Richard, Duke of York

Edward IV

Richard, Duke of Gloucester

Richard Neville, Earl of Warwick

Henry Tudor

Margaret of Anjou

Dissolve from one person to the next after each story

2 The researcher has found ten details about each person. This is too much information for your audience, so select five or six details from each list to include in your script.

HENRY VI
1. dates 1421–71
2. became king in 1422
3. founded Eton College and King's College, Cambridge
4. in 1437, old enough to rule on his own
5. son, Edward, born in October 1453
6. mentally ill and incapable of ruling for some time
7. fled to France after Yorkist victories in 1462
8. restored to the throne by the Earl of Warwick in 1470
9. murdered in the Tower in 1471
10. character: saintly, weak leader, unsuited to be king

EDWARD IV
1. dates 1442–83
2. eldest son of Richard, Duke of York
3. crowned Edward IV in June 1461
4. had problems controlling the Earl of Warwick
5. secretly married Elizabeth Woodville
6. when Warwick changed sides, Edward fled to France
7. defeated and killed Warwick at the Battle of Barnet
8. after 1471, his reign was mainly peaceful
9. died suddenly in 1483 of natural causes
10. character: popular, brave

RICHARD, DUKE OF YORK
1. dates 1411–60
2. descended from Edward III
3. cousin of Henry VI
4. served Henry VI as Lieutenant of France
5. served Henry VI as Lieutenant of Ireland
6. ruled as Protector of England, 1454–55
7. ruled as Protector of England, 1455–56
8. became heir to the throne in 1460
9. killed at the Battle of Wakefield
10. character: ambitious, fair

RICHARD, DUKE OF GLOUCESTER
1. dates 1452–85
2. fought bravely to help his brother, Edward become king
3. made Duke of Gloucester in 1461
4. may have murdered Henry VI and others
5. took the throne in 1483
6. put down revolts against him
7. imprisoned his nephews in the Tower
8. killed at the Battle of Bosworth in 1485
9. last English king to die on the battlefield
10. character: brave, ruthless

RICHARD NEVILLE, EARL OF WARWICK
1. dates 1428–71
2. nephew of the Duke of York
3. known as 'the king maker'
4. helped Edward to become king in 1461
5. gave advice to Edward IV
6. Edward IV did not always follow his advice
7. tried to help Edward IV's brother to become king
8. placed Henry VI back on the throne in 1470
9. killed at the Battle of Barnet in 1471
10. character: generous, arrogant, hot-tempered

HENRY TUDOR
1. dates 1457–1509
2. his father, Edmund Tudor, died of plague in 1456
3. brought up by his uncle, Jasper Tudor
4. became Earl of Richmond in 1456
5. fled to France in 1471
6. landed with a small force at Milford Haven in 1485
7. became King Henry VII after the Battle of Bosworth in 1485
8. first of the Tudor monarchs
9. married Elizabeth, the daughter of Edward IV
10. character: clever, good organiser, good with money

MARGARET OF ANJOU
1. dates 1430–82
2. fifth child of the Count of Anjou, France
3. married Henry VI in 1445, aged 15
4. son, Prince Edward of Lancaster, born in 1453
5. used her limited power as queen to fight for the Lancastrian cause
6. won the second Battle of St Albans in 1461
7. fled to France with Henry after Yorkist victory in 1462
8. defeated at Tewkesbury and imprisoned 1471–75 by Edward VI; her son killed
9. died in poverty in France in 1482
10. character: learned, determined

How do we know **what we know**?

There are lots of history books about the Wars of the Roses. But where do historians get their information from? Another major source of evidence about the Wars of the Roses is a collection of documents known as the Paston Letters.

The Pastons were a family from Norfolk. Some of them were landowners. Others were lawyers, soldiers or even members of Parliament. The Pastons owned Caister Castle on the coast, east of Norwich. It was one of the first castles built of brick in England. It was besieged in 1469.

SOURCE A

'... your brother and his men stand in great danger at Caister, and are short of food. Some are dead and others badly hurt, and gunpowder and arrows are lacking. The place is badly broken down by the guns of the other party, so that, unless they have hasty help, they are likely to lose both their lives and the place.'

About the siege, from a letter written by Margaret Paston

There are portraits of most of the important people involved. There is also archaeological evidence for some of the battles. Many of the castles belonging to the nobles who fought in the wars still exist. There is also evidence from documents that were produced at the time or soon afterwards.

For a long time people believed the story of the Wars of the Roses given in Shakespeare's plays. Here is a well-known extract from the play, *Richard III*. The scene shows the death of Richard at the Battle of Bosworth.

SOURCE B

Act 5.
Another part of the field [the Battle of Bosworth 1485]

Enter KING RICHARD

KING RICHARD:	*A horse! a horse! my kingdom for a horse!*
CATESBY:	*Withdraw, my lord! I'll help you to a horse.*
KING RICHARD :	*Slave, I have set my life upon a cast,*
	And I will stand the hazard of the die:
	I think there be six Richmonds in the field:
	Five have I slain to-day instead of him.
	A horse! a horse! my kingdom for a horse!
	Exit

Enter, from opposite sides, KING RICHARD and RICHMOND [Henry Tudor];
and exit fighting. Retreat and flourish. Then re-enter RICHMOND, with STANLEY
[Thomas, Lord Stanley] bearing the crown, and other Lords and soldiers

RICHMOND:	*God and your arms be prais'd, victorious friends;*
	The day is ours, the bloody dog is dead.

END

Finding out about
The Wars of the Roses

1. Work out what happens in this extract from the play.

2. Draw simple storyboard sketches to show the action (stick figures are fine for this). Write camera directions and captions for your sketches.

3. What does Source A tell us about the fighting?

4. Draw a storyboard with two simple pictures to illustrate the action. Add camera directions and captions.

5. Think about where you could use this in your final TV programme.

....

However, can you trust Shakespeare as a source of evidence here? Read the information box below before you decide.
(Clue: think of 'Chinese whispers'.)

How did Shakespeare know?

Shakespeare was born nearly 100 years after the wars finished. He used history books to help him write his plays about Henry VI and Richard III. The authors of those history books may have spoken to survivors of the wars.

Shakespeare did a lot of research for his plays. Before writing *Richard III*, he had probably read Sir Thomas More's, *Life of Richard III* and chronicles written by Edward Halle and Raphael Holinshed.

Thomas More was only a child at the time of the Battle of Bosworth. However, he spent his childhood in the home of a man who was present at many of the events described in his book. Both of the other authors used the work of earlier historians.

6. Would you use any extracts from Shakespeare's plays in your TV programme? Give reasons for your answer.

7. Is there a good reason to include a play extract even if you think it might not be true? Explain why you think that.

The two Margarets

In the 15th Century, a married woman's goods all belonged to her husband. She could not make a will without his permission. A girl from a wealthy family could expect to have her husband chosen for her. She had to know how to dance, ride and do needlework. At that time, only a widow had any kind of independence.

Despite all this, women played an important part in the Wars of the Roses. In medieval times, families often followed armies to war. Women helped prepare food and look after the wounded. Sometimes they played a more active role. When the enemy attacked, Lady Knyvet said she would rather die than let her castle be captured. She did not die and she kept her castle!

One famous lady in the story of the Wars of the Roses was Margaret Beaufort. Her second husband was Edmund Tudor. Their son, Henry Tudor, later became King Henry VII. Her fourth husband was Thomas, Lord Stanley. Margaret helped persuade Stanley to help Henry Tudor win the Battle of Bosworth and become king.

Perhaps the most impressive woman involved in the Wars of the Roses was Margaret of Anjou. You have already come across her. After her husband, Henry VI became ill, she gradually took over as the real leader of the Lancastrians. She was captured at the Battle of Tewkesbury and imprisoned in the Tower until 1475. Margaret died in France in 1482.

Margaret Beaufort

Finding out about the Wars of the Roses

1. In your TV programme, you need to show that women were important during the Wars of the Roses, even if they did not actually fight. Draw a set of storyboards and write the script for this section of your programme. When writing your script, remember to:
   - avoid unnecessary detail
   - write about one thing at a time
   - do not assume your audience already knows things
   - remember you are writing for a narrator, not writing a story.

2. You have almost finished planning your TV programme, but there are still a few things left to think about. You have storyboards and a script for most of the programme. But is there anything missing? For example, have you explained why the fighting is known as the Wars of the Roses?

*Margaret
of Anjou*

Why is it called the Wars of the Roses?

Most historians think that the term 'Wars of
the Roses' was not used until 1829. However, the
idea was included in one of Shakespeare's plays.
There is a garden scene where red and white
roses are used to show if characters support
York or Lancaster. The Yorkists did use a white
rose on some of their flags, but it was just one of
a number of symbols, not the main one.

Finding out about the Wars of the Roses

1 Decide on the final title for your TV
programme.

2 Read the information in the panel and add
a section on why the struggles are called
the 'Wars of the Roses' to your storyboards
and script.

3 Look at the sections in your programme
again.

- Why the fighting started
- Soldiers and war
- Who was involved?
- How do we know what
  we know?
- Women in the Wars of
  the Roses
- Why it is called the Wars
  of the Roses

Are these sections in the clearest order?
Decide if you want to make any changes
and then rewrite the list.

4 If there are any points you think are
missing from your script, now is the time
for any extra research and writing. Use
the Internet, encyclopaedias or reference
books to add additional details to each
section of your script and storyboards.

5 With a partner, review your finished script
and storyboards. Make any changes
that you think will improve the final
programme.

Medieval **inventions**

It is easy to get the idea that not much changed during the medieval period – that life was not much different between the death of King Harold at Hastings in 1066 and the death of King Richard at Bosworth in 1485. In fact, a lot of the things we take for granted today first appeared in England during the medieval period.

SOURCE A

SOURCE B

SOURCE C

SOURCE D

SOURCE E

SOURCE F

SOURCE G

SOURCE H

ACTIVITIES

1. Match one of the captions below to each one of the sources here. Each date in the captions shows when we have the first evidence of that invention. It could already have been in use for some years.

Caption	Source, by letter
Cannon, 1320	
Clock, 1325	
Compass, 1190	
Post windmill, 1185	
Rudder, 1250	
Spectacles, 1285	
Spinning wheel, 1250	
Wheelbarrow, 1200	

2. Write out the list of inventions again. This time start with the one that you think did most to change people's lives and finish with the one you think had least impact.

3. Write sentences to explain your first and last choices.

Pulling things together

From working through this book you will know now that history is about people. These people may have been monarchs, ministers, maids or miners: anyone, in fact, whether their name has been recorded in a history book or not!

Here are some of the people you will have met while you have been studying history. Have at look at each picture and caption, and then have a go at the activities.

William I, who won the Battle of Hastings

Henry II, who ruled England and most of France

Thomas Becket, who was murdered in Canterbury Cathedral

Wat Tyler, who was leader of the Peasants' Revolt

Richard III, who was killed at the Battle of Bosworth

William Wallace, the Scottish hero

Henry VII, who won the Battle of Bosworth

John Ball, who preached that everyone was equal

Richard II, who ended the Peasants' Revolt

Edward I, who conquered Wales

Eleanor of Aquitaine, Queen of England, who rebelled against her husband

Countess of Leicester, whose account book tells us so much about medieval life

William of Long Sutton, the peasant who shared his life story with us

Robin Hood, who may have robbed the rich to help the poor

ACTIVITIES

1. Write out the list of names in chronological (date) order. Try to do this without checking in the book first.

2. Write down the name, or anything you can remember, of people you have studied in history, who are not shown on this page. Try to do this without checking in the book first.

3. Write out the names of five people you have studied, who you think should be remembered most. Write a sentence or two to explain your choices.

4. Robin Hood does not appear in this book. Can you explain why?

5. Pick two people you have studied, who are not on this page but who you think deserve to be remembered.

6. Playing cards were just coming into use in medieval times. Sometimes they showed information about events and people. Produce a set of cards for five people you have studied this year who particularly impress you. Write five bullet points about the person on each card.

King Harold

- reigned 1066
- said to have promised he would help William become king
- became king after Edward the Confessor
- defeated Harald Hadrada in 1066
- killed at the Battle of Hastings by the Normans.

1066 – 1485

Interpreting the past

How do historians interpret the past?

Historians use evidence to make sense of the past. In this book we have used many different types of evidence – archaeological, physical, visual and written. Each piece of evidence gives a version of something that happened in the past. But some of that evidence has been **inconclusive** and some has been contradictory. Much more evidence has been lost since the events or is difficult to use.

So, how do historians select which evidence to use, and which not to use? How do they build up a picture of what happened in the past?

All historians bring their own experiences, interests and ideas to their study of history. Some are more interested in political history (*Kings, Queens and Governments*), some in social history (*everyday life*). Others prefer economic history (*to do with money*) or even religious history. This is why historians' interpretations of the past differ so much.

Here is our interpretation, as authors of this book, of Medieval Times. See if you agree.

ACTIVITIES

1. What interpretation of Medieval Times are we, the authors, presenting to you?

2. Which type of history do you think we are most interested in?

3. Choose *three* images that you think show **your** interpretation of Medieval Times. They might be from this page, or elsewhere in the book, or they might be from another source altogether. Explain your choice to a partner. Does their selection agree with yours? You could even make a display for your classroom wall.

NEW WORDS

Inconclusive
Leading to no final result

123

Glossary

Abbot
Head of an abbey or monastery

Allegiance
Loyalty to a leader, a country or a belief

Alliance
Agreement to work together

Anachronism
Something that didn't exist at that time, e.g. television

Angevin
A person from Anjou, a region of France. Associated with the Plantagenet kings of England

Angevin
From Anjou

Archaeological evidence
Actual remains from historical periods found in the ground

Barbican
Fortified gateway, on the way into a castle

Barricade
A barrier to stop the movement of a crowd or army

Bastard castles
Unlawful. Built without the Kings permission

Besieged
To be surrounded in a castle by attackers wanting its surrender

Campaign
Series of battles

Canon law
Church law

Cesspit
Pit for sewage

Chastity
To never have sex or marry

Civil War
A war between different groups in the same country

Clamoured
Made a loud noise

Clergy
People with religious duties

Colonies
Countries controlled by another country

Concentric
Made of circles inside each other

Confiscated
Take something away in punishment

Constable
Person in charge of a castle and responsible to the lord for its safety

Constitution
Rules and guidelines for governing a state

Convulsion
Violent, uncontrollable movement of the body

Cottager
Person who had no land or rights

Courtier
Adviser to the king

Crusade
A holy war, backed by the Pope

Crusade
Holy war, blessed by the Pope

Daub
Mixture of clay and straw pushed into wattle

Democracy
Type of government in which ordinary people vote and have some power

Dialogue
Speech

Diplomacy
Working out problems without fighting

Disbanded
Sent home

Dowry
Payment to a husband on marriage

Duke
Very important ruler of a territory, nearly as powerful as a king

Earl
Important and powerful landowner in England

Enchantment
Using 'magic' to win

Excommunicating
Throwing someone out of the Church

Fallow
Field left unsown

Freeman
Person who rents land from a lord

Harrow
Break down the soil after ploughing

Hawking
Hunting with a hawk

Higgledy-piggledy
All over the place

Holy relics
Remains of an important holy person or object, thought to have great power

Homage
Acknowledging someone as lord

Housecarls
Member of very best Saxon troops, usually used as a bodyguard by Harold and the earls

Hundred
a part of a county or shire, with its own court

Illegitimate
Person born when their parents are not married

Illustrious
Well-known and admired person

Keep
Strongest tower of a castle

Laying waste
Destroying everything

Looted
Stole goods from an enemy

Martyr
A person who is killed or punished for their beliefs

Mass
Church service including Holy Communion

Mercenary
Soldier who fights for whoever pays

Mint
Place where coins are made

Mitre
Archbishop's hat and sign of his position

Motte and bailey
Mound (motte) that a castle was built on; courtyard (bailey) around the castle

Oath
Promise, often made in the name of God and considered very important at the time

Omen
Event that suggests something good or bad is going to happen

Overlord
Ruler of lords

Pallet
Mattress

Parliament
Body of elected representatives responsible for running a country

Patriot
Someone who loves their country and is willing to defend it

Pedlar
Traveling seller of small items

Penance
Punishment for a sin

Perfidious
Someone who cannot be trusted

Pestilence
The plague, Black Death

Physician
Trained doctor

Pilgrimage
Religious journey to a holy place

Pillage
Steal

Poll tax
A tax paid by adults

Preach
Give a religious talk

Preserve
Prepare food for storage

Rebellion
Attempt to get rid of a king or ruler

Regent
Person who rules until a king is old enough to rule for himself

Rushlight
Reeds dipped in mutton fat

Sacked
Robbed and destroyed

Sanitation
Toilets and sewers

Saxons
People who lived in England before the arrival of the Normans

Scuttage
Tax paid to the king instead of providing knights to fight for him

Siege
An attempt to force a castle or town to surrender by surrounding it and cutting off supplies

Slaughter
Kill

Symptom
Feature of a disease

Tanner
A craftsman who works with leather

Tenant
Person who rents land from a lord

Thatcher
Person who makes roofs from straw

Thresh
Remove the grains from the straw

Tithe
A tax of 10% of income paid by everyone to the Church

Traitor
Person who goes against the king

Treasury
Place where the governments money was kept

Trial by Ordeal
A persons guilt or innocence was tested by a painful or dangerous ordeal such as being thrown into deep water or holding a burning hot iron bar

Tyranny
Cruelty

Vat
A large container for storing liquid

Vengeance
The worst punishment

Villein
Person who worked unpaid for the lord in return for a small plot of land

Wattle
Fence of woven twigs

Welsh Marcher Lord
Lords on the Welsh borders, given land and power for keeping the peace and controlling the area

Index

The Rob Walker Racing Team

Dorking's part in Motor Racing History

Tom Loftus

Foreword by Robbie Walker

THE
COCKEREL
PRESS

ISBN 978-1-909871-12-0

The Cockerel Press is part of the Dorking Museum and Heritage Centre, The Old Foundry, 62 West Street, Dorking RH4 1BS.

Printed and bound by Short Run Press Limited, Exeter

www.dorkingmuseum.org.uk

Enquiries: admin@dorkingmuseum.org.uk

Contents

Introduction

Acknowledgements

Foreword by Robbie Walker

The Rob Walker Racing Team

Introduction

Glance through any book on the history of motor racing and the achievements of the Rob Walker Racing Team, or the RRC Walker Racing Team, to give it its official title, will feature.

Rob Walker was the first, and will almost certainly be the last, private team owner or 'privateer' to win a Formula One World Championship Grand Prix. And he did it not once, but nine times between 1958 and 1968, a period regarded by many as the sport's golden years. His team was also very successful in many other categories of motorsport, including F2, F3, sports car racing and hill climbs.

Rob Walker at the 1969 German Grand Prix.

As a 'private entrant' the team did not construct its own cars, but bought them direct from manufacturers, be it Lotus, Cooper or Connaught. The cars were then prepared for racing in the team's workshop, based in the quiet Surrey market town of Dorking. There they were adapted by the top mechanics of the day including Alf Francis, John Chisman, Stan Collier, Tim Wall and Tony Cleverly. World renowned drivers like Stirling Moss, Jack Brabham, Jo Siffert and Graham Hill then travelled to Dorking to finalise their seating position and other details. The cars were finished in the team's distinctive colours of dark blue with a white stripe around the nose, in recognition of Rob Walker's Scottish roots, and transported from Dorking to races all over the world. Although the team was small, and seen by many as the perpetual underdog, it became the bane of the works' teams, particularly the mighty Ferrari. This was a reputation which Rob and the team enjoyed immensely.

A book of this length can only give an overview of Rob Walker's life and achievements in motorsport. Extensive accounts of team activities can the found in the books listed in Appendix 2 and I would encourage you to discover more about Dorking's part in motor racing history.

Tom Loftus
Dorking
July 2018

Acknowledgements

During my research for this book I have been fortunate to meet some wonderful people, and I would like to thank them all for giving their time so generously. In particular I would like to thank Rob Walker's son, Robbie, Tony and Sue Cleverly, Jim Chisman, Eric Mansfield, Rob Rennie and Sue and Arthur Somerville. A big thanks for all the support and encouragement from the Dorking Museum and the Cockerel Press team. Also thank you to Kathy Atherton for all her guidance with this book and the exhibition. Additional research was carried out courtesy of the Brooklands Museum and the Haynes International Motor Museum. I would also like to thank my wife Ali and the rest of my family for their support and patience.

Many thanks to Robbie Walker, Tony Cleverly, Jim Chisman, Rob Rennie, Stewart Booth, Royston Williamson, The Dorking Museum and The Signature Store for permission to reproduce images. All efforts have been made to contact the copyright holders of the images used but in some instances this has not been possible to identify. Please get in touch with the Cockerel Press if you own copyright to an un-credited image so that we can amend future editions.

This book is based on an exhibition at Dorking Museum from September 2018 to January 2019 which celebrated the twin anniversaries of the teams first and last Formula One World Championship Grand Prix wins in 1958 and 1968. The exhibition also marked the centenary of Rob Walker's birth in August 1917.

I am, of course, enormously proud of my father's heritage. But, memories are short lived. When the Dorking Museum and the Dorking Town Partnership announced their intention of holding an exhibition and a Rob Walker Tribute Day, I was thrilled that they should choose to honour my father so many years later.

For the past two years Tom Loftus, Rob Rennie and the Dorking Town Partnership have been working tirelessly to make these events happen. Apart from the endless red tape, they have assembled an amazing number of the team's cars. Records, memorabilia and former personnel have been traced for a wonderful exhibition at the Dorking Museum. Together with this book, it provides a fascinating potted history of my father's life and his motor racing career. To them, along with their fellow helpers, I would like to say a huge thank you.

Besides all the teams' successes in other classes, this event celebrates 60 years since his first World Championship victory in Argentina and 50 since his last: the British Grand Prix at Brands Hatch. Few F1 fans today would believe that a little privately owned outfit could win 9 GPs including Monaco three times. It truly was a family business pitted against the might of the factory teams.

Dorking was the centre of Rob Walker Racing. Complicated administration, engines and gearboxes assembled, cars built, strategies planned with many a famous driver. It was a hive of activity year round, but it was also a haven where mechanics and cars returned after noisy and hectic races.

Pippbrook also catered for the everyday motorist. It evolved from a petrol station to a successful Ford agency and service centre. Probably because of the racing connection, many took their sports cars to be tuned. Post service, these had to be road tested and it was obligatory to take the Mickleham bends at 100mph! Not all returned in the same condition!

Rob loved going to Dorking and it held a soft spot in his memory for many years after he had moved on. Pippbrook held a big place in my heart too ... as my childhood was full of the exploits coming from there ... it was every schoolboy's dream to have a winning racing team in the family and I still remember the thrill of visiting the workshops, seeing the cars and talking to the mechanics.

Such memories

Robbie Walker

London

July 2018

Chapter 1

The Gentleman Racer

Robert Ramsey Campbell Walker was born on 14th August 1917, into a privileged life as a member of the Johnnie Walker whiskey family. His lifelong fascination with motor racing started at the tender age of seven, when, whilst on holiday in France, he saw his first motor race at Boulogne-sur-Mer. On his eleventh birthday he was given his first car, a 1924 bull-nosed Morris Coupe. He soon learned to drive (and race) the Morris along the mile-long drive up to Sutton Veny House, the Walker family home near Warminster in Wiltshire.

Rob and his first car, a bull-nosed Morris Coupe.

School Days

Rob was educated at Sherborne School in Dorset and at Magdalene College, Cambridge where he was described as undisciplined and rebellious. While at Cambridge he learnt to fly with the University Air Squadron. However, he was banned for life soon after for 'jumping' all the fences at the Cottenham point to point course in a Tiger Moth during the lunch interval. Rob spent his summers playing cricket for his college and later became a playing member of the MCC. Despite his total lack of interest in academia he managed to obtain a degree in geography.

By his 21st birthday he had owned 21 cars, including a couple of unwieldy Rolls Royce cars his mother bought for him in a vain attempt to slow him down. In 1938 he met his future wife, Elizabeth (Betty) Duncan, who was studying painting in Paris. At around the same time he met the second love of his life.

Rob at Cambridge with his supercharged 1929 Alvis.

Rob, number 10, racing his Delahaye at Brooklands in 1937.

Rob the wheel of his Delahaye at the Tertre Rouge corner during the 1939 Le Mans 24 hour race.

He was strolling down London's Park Lane when he saw a Delahaye Type 35 sports car in a showroom with a £400 price ticket on the bonnet. His yearly Cambridge allowance was only £360, but the salesman introduced Rob to a wonderful thing called 'hire purchase', and with only a signature the car was his.

Brooklands

In the late 1930s Rob made his competition debut at the Lewes Speed Trials, driving a supercharged Lea-Francis Ulster sports car. Soon he was making regular journeys from Cambridge to Surrey to race the Delahaye at the Brooklands race track. The car was very quick and took part in an event, instigated by an article in Autocar magazine, to determine 'The Fastest Car in Britain'. Rob did not race himself but enlisted Arthur Dobson, a renowned driver of the day. Over two races at Brooklands the Delahaye was declared the winner on aggregate. Though he also loaned the car to Prince Bira of Siam (another famous driver) for a race at Crystal Palace, he usually drove the car himself, and as often as he could. It was the era of the 'gentlemen racers' and Rob enjoyed the whole experience immensely.

Le Mans

In 1939 Rob fulfilled a childhood dream when he entered his Delahaye in the world-famous 24-hour sports car race at Le Mans with Ian Connell as co-driver. For his evening driving stint Rob, always the gentleman, chose to wear a dark blue pinstripe suit, before changing the next morning into an informal Prince of Wales' check.

A broken exhaust during the race made the car's footwell scorching hot and burnt Connell's feet so badly that he was unable to continue. Rob took over and drove a twelve-hour stint to the finish, soaking his rope-soled shoes in water at each stop to keep his feet cool.

Near the end of the race his pit crew, which included Count Doric Heydon as team manager, called him in for a glass of champagne to give him energy, guilty that they were down to the last bottle. Rob finally crossed the line in eighth place overall and third in his class. The Delahaye had run for 24 hours without a change of tyres at an average speed of 78 mph. After the race Rob drove straight to a Paris night club where he celebrated with other British drivers until ten o'clock the following morning!

Rob raced the Delahaye until the outbreak of war in September 1939. He was in France the day before war was declared, negotiating his starting money for a cancelled race. He just managed to catch the last channel crossing back to England for six years.

Walker goes to War

Rob joined the Royal Navy and trained to be a Fleet Air Arm Pilot. A desperate shortage of experienced pilots meant that his earlier flying misdemeanour was not mentioned. In fact he was congratulated on his flying ability and later commissioned as a Sub-Lieutenant RNVR. During his service career he flew a variety of aircraft including Gladiators, Swordfish and Hurricanes.

Sub-Lieutenant (A) R.R.C. Walker RNVR.

In 1940 Rob Walker and Betty Duncan were married at St. Peter's church in Eaton Square, London. Rob promised his new wife that he would end his racing career, though he probably thought that he was unlikely to survive the war anyway. But he survived the torpedoing of HMS Cleopatra whilst supporting the invasion of Sicily and later saw service in the Far East. He arrived back in London on 8th May 1945, just in time to join Betty in Trafalgar Square for the VE Day celebrations.

Betty Walker and Rob's Coupe des Alpes Delahaye in the late 1930s. The car was given to Rob on his 21st birthday.

Chapter 2

1940s Getting Into Gear

Rob was 28 when he was demobbed, and eager to indulge his passion for fast cars and motor racing. Honouring his promise to Betty not to race himself, he confined his driving activities to the occasional hill climb or sprint. But he wanted to be close to the action. He decided to become a 'private entrant' and to manage his own racing team.

Rob still owned his pre-war Delahaye and he went into partnership as owner/manager with driver/mechanic Guy Jason-Henry. Post-war petrol rationing meant that there were limited opportunities for organised car racing, but when they did enter a race Jason-Henry won. Despite its age, the Delahaye was one of the fastest road racing cars in Britain post-war.

Rob and his Delahaye in 1945

In 1947 Rob bought the Pippbrook Garage in Dorking and then acquired a collection of workshops in nearby London Road. This would become the base for the fledgling Rob Walker Racing Team.

Why Dorking?

A small market town in Surrey may seem an odd location to set-up a motor racing team. However, back in 1906 the world's first purpose-built racing circuit, Brooklands, had opened in Weybridge and Surrey had become the focus for Britain's pioneering racing car industry. In later years world championship winning teams like Brabham (based in Chessington), Cooper (in Surbiton), Tyrell (in Ockham) and McLaren (in Woking) continued this legacy. So, for Rob Walker Dorking provided the perfect location to attract the skilled mechanics and drivers he required to join his fledgling racing team.

The Pippbrook Garage soon after its opening in 1931, with its first owner John Lloyd.

The Pippbrook Garage

The original Pippbrook Garage had been built in 1931 in the contemporary Art Deco style with funds provided by the parents of its first owner, John Alexander Lloyd (III). Coincidentally, Lloyd was an enthusiastic car racer. Situated in a prime location on the newly completed Deepdene Avenue (A24), the garage proved popular with local motorists during the 1930s and 40s.

1937 aerial photograph showing the Pippbrook Garage, house and mill. ©Historic England

BY ORDER OF CALDWELL'S GARAGES, Ltd.

Re G. M. Caldwell, deceased.

THE PIPPBROOK GARAGE
DORKING, SURREY.

For Sale by Auction, unless previously sold,
at the Red Lion Hotel, Dorking, Surrey, on
Friday, 25th July, 1947, at 3 p.m. punctually.

Solicitors :

Messrs. ATKINS, WALTER & LOCKE,

316, High Street, Dorking.

And at 26/28 High Street, Guildford, and 1029 London Road, Thornton Heath.

Joint Auctioneers :

Messrs. GODDARD, DAVISON & SMITH, LTD., The Motor & General Auction Mart, 70, Seymour Place, London, W.1.	Messrs. CUBITT & WEST, London Road, Dorking. Effingham ; Farnham ; Haslemere ; Hindhead.

Following the death of the then owner, G. M. Caldwell, in 1947, the garage, with its four petrol pumps and workshop, was put up for auction. The auction was held at The Red Lion Hotel* in Dorking on Friday 25th July 1947 and Rob Walker made a successful offer. Much later he would expand his business interests, acquiring several other garages, including one at Crosley, near Warminster in Wiltshire, from which he operated a Lotus dealership.

*The Red Lion Hotel was situated next to Lloyds Bank in the High Street until the site was redeveloped in 1960s.

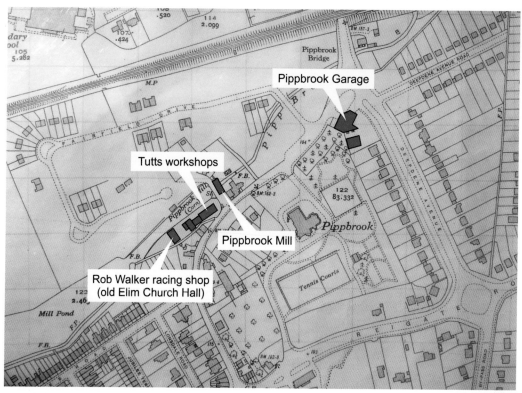

1938 Ordnance Survey map of the Pippbrook area.

London Road Workshops

To provide an operating base for his racing team Rob purchased a nearby collection of buildings and workshops. Situated on a small triangular piece of land opposite Pippbrook Mill, between London Road and Fairfield Drive, the buildings included the old Elim Church Hall which became the team's main racing shop. The site had previously been occupied by H R Nash, who built motorcycles, small 3-wheeled tractors and mowers.

Pippbrook Mill

Straddling the Pipp Brook, a tributary of the River Mole, Pippbrook Mill had been constructed on the site of the 11th century East Mill in 1792, but flour production had ceased in 1932. In the 1970s it housed the Rhino Studios where local bands, amongst them The Cure, rehearsed and recorded. The grade II listed building suffered a serious fire in 1979 but was totally rebuilt to its original design.

Ready to go Racing

By the late 1940s Rob was in a position to start building his team. In 1949 he entered his faithful Delahaye in the first post-war Le Mans 24-Hour race. Tony Rolt was brought in as Jason-Henry's co-driver. During the war Rolt escaped seven times from German prisoner-of-war camps before eventually being sent to Colditz Castle. In early 1944, he was one of the masterminds behind the audacious glider escape plan.

ROB WALKER RACING TEAM

PIPPBROOK GARAGE, LONDON ROAD, DORKING, SURREY   TELEPHONE 2871

Unfortunately, the engine's main bearings failed while the pair were in fifth place and their race was over by midnight. A third place at the French Grand Prix followed, after which Rob decided to sell the Delahaye. Years later, in the 1970s, Walker bought the car again. Fully restored, it is now on display at the Haynes International Motor Museum in Sparkford, near Yeovil.

Tony Rolt continued to drive for Rob Walker until 1954. Jason-Henry, on the other hand, took a different path. Unbeknownst to Rob, Jason-Henry fitted a false petrol tank to Rob's Delahaye in France. He was apprehended by customs at Newhaven smuggling 3,000 watches. A completely blameless Rob had to pay £400 to retrieve the impounded car.

Tutts London Road workshops, behind which Rob Walker operated his racing team for twenty years. (Tutts of Dorking)

Chapter 3

1950s The Giantkillers

n the early 1950s the top drivers competed regularly, not just in Formula One races, but also in Formula Two and Three, and in other forms of motorsport, including saloon car racing. They were true professionals who would race just about anything on four wheels! But there was considerably less money in the sport than there is today. Drivers' pay was good compared to the average wage, but nowhere near the multimillion pound salaries of today's superstars. Drivers were paid a race fee for every event they entered, so the more races they entered, the more money they made. The fee was calculated on the driver's previous results and popularity and his ability to pull in the crowds.

There was little or no advertising on the cars, which were traditionally painted in the national colours of the team's home country: British racing green for the UK based teams, red for Italy, silver for Germany and light blue for France. In recognition of his Scottish roots, Rob chose to paint his cars dark blue with a white roundel and stripe across the nose to echo the Scottish flag.

1950 Season

Louis Chiron in the Delage at Indianapolis in 1929. Chiron holds the record as the oldest driver to race in Formula One. In 1955 at the age of 55, he finished 6th in the Monaco Grand Prix.

In 1950 Rob bought a couple of pre-war Delage single-seater racing cars. The first was a runner, which Rob had modified with an ERA engine and was raced by Tony Rolt until 1952. The second chassis was not in running condition and was originally bought for spare parts, but Rob later found that this car had a celebrated racing history. A 1927 model with a 2½ litre supercharged straight-eight engine, it had finished in seventh place at the 1929 Indianapolis 500, with Louis Chiron at the wheel. It was later raced to several victories by the legendary English driver Richard Seaman.

Tony Rolt (number 18) powers the ERA Delage off the line at Goodwood.

Rob decided that the car was too historic to break-up for spares, and it was beautifully restored to its original condition at Pippbrook by mechanic John Chisman. The Delage was much-loved and remained in Rob's private collection until the 1980s. There was, however, one major problem associated with working on a Delage at Pippbrook: the noise. The cars were so loud that when the mechanics fired up the engine they would take bets on how long it would take for the neighbours to call to complain.

May 1950 saw the first ever Drivers' World Championship Formula One Race at Silverstone, but the Walker team was not in a position to enter the race. The Delage gave the team its first sample of single-seater racing later the same year when Tony Rolt drove in the International Trophy at Silverstone.

1951-1952 Seasons

In the spring of 1951 Rob acquired an ex-works Aston Martin DB2 sports car, registration plate 'VMF 65'. The car was driven by George Abecassis in the 1951 British Empire Trophy race at Douglas, Isle of Man, and later by Rob himself at speed trials in Ramsgate and Brighton. The car was also driven by Tony Rolt, Peter Collins, Roy Salvadri and Eric Thompson, who won at Snetterton in May 1952. After a series of wins at various other speed trials, Rob finally sold this celebrated car in 1955. In 2010 'VMF 65' was sold at auction for over half a million pounds!

During this period, Rob entered the Delage in the 1951 Goodwood F1 Trophy (where Tony Rolt finished in 3rd place), the 1951 Ulster Trophy at Dundrod (where Peter Walker finished in 8th

Following the team's first F1 victory in the 1953 Coronation Trophy race at Crystal Palace, Tony Rolt's F2 Connaught and the winners' cup are paraded around Dorking. The photo was taken outside the Spotted Dog in South Street and the small banner on the trailer reads 'Success!'. (Robbie Walker)

Alf Francis and Tony Cleverly working on the bodywork of a Cooper at Pippbrook. (Robbie Walker)

place), the 1951 International Trophy at Silverstone (where Rolt finished 7th), and the 1952 Richmond Trophy at Goodwood (where Rolt retired).

1953 Season - First Formula One Race

A Connaught A-Type Formula Two single-seater was next to arrive at Pippbrook. It proved a very successful car, winning 16 out of 24 races entered during the year, including the team's first international victory in the Coronation Trophy at the Crystal Palace track in South London. It was driven by Tony Rolt in the 1953 British Grand Prix, Rob's first world championship Formula One race, but was forced to retire on lap 70 out of 90 when the car's half -shaft failed.

1954 Season

A 2½ litre B-Type Connaught was bought to compete in the 1954 Formula One season but it required a lot of attention from the mechanics. Rob also signed Peter Collins, his first truly professional driver. The team's only Formula One race, the British Grand Prix at Silverstone, ended in retirement.

1955 Season

Tony Cleverly (right) joined the Pippbrook Garage in 1955 as a 16-year-old school-leaver and soon became involved in the racing team. He was soon spending evenings and weekends working on Jack Fairman's Connaught. Tony's first overseas Grand Prix involved a tortuous 32-hour flight. To prepare a car for a race he and the team would sometimes have to work long hours and a 24-hour stint was not uncommon. Later, under the watchful eye of Alf Francis, who was very helpful to the youngster, he began to develop and strengthen his engineering skills.

He was also involved in some hairy moments, including a high-flying incident on the starting grid of the Canadian Grand Prix. Jo Siffert was on pole and, unknown to Tony

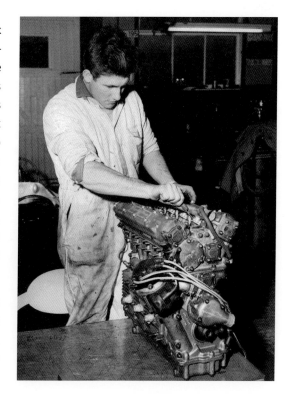

(who was still working at the back of Siffert's car), decided to do a practice start. Before he knew what was happening, Tony found himself flying through the air when his legs were caught between Siffert's fast-turning wheels and the rear wheels of the car next to it. He landed on his head and later recalled little of the race.

Rob entered Tony Rolt and Peter Walker (no relation) for the 1955 British Grand Prix at Aintree, but they were both forced to retire their Connaughts from the race. The team did manage to win one race that season, when Peter Walker took victory at a non-championship event at Snetterton.

1956-1957 Seasons

For the 1956 season Rob arranged for Tony Brooks to drive a Formula Two Cooper. He was partnered by Reg Parnell in the Connaught. But Parnell broke a collar-bone in a heavy crash while driving the Connaught at Crystal Palace. In 1957, equipped with a pair of Coventry-Climax powered F2 Cooper T41s, the team embarked on its first full international competition season. It achieved its first Formula One finish when the future world champion, Australian Jack Brabham, finished in seventh place at the Pescara Grand Prix in the Abruzzo region of Italy.

At Monaco, with just five laps to go, Brabham was running in a strong third when the fuel pump fell off his Cooper and he coasted to a halt. Determined to finish the race, Brabham famously pushed his car to the chequered flag to claim a hard-earned sixth place.

Australian Jack Brabham, who won the world drivers' championship in 1959, 1960 and 1966.

1958 Season - The Taste of Victory

Prospects for 1958 took a turn for the better when Stirling Moss agreed to drive for the Pippbrook team. French Champion Maurice Trintignant joined as the number two driver. The deals were sealed with nothing more than a handshake. Rob also hired the highly experienced Alf Francis, Stirling's preferred mechanic and the three of them went on to form a successful team. Over the coming years Rob and Stirling's relationship would grow strong, with each having a mutual respect for each other.

John Chisman sitting in the ex-Richard Seaman Delage which he rebuilt twice. The car's original restoration was completed by John in 1964 and the second rebuild followed a fire at Pippbrook in 1968, more of which later. Like Tony, John started working at the Pippbrook garage before joining the racing team in 1958. He was a highly skilled mechanic and became an integral part of the team. (Jim Chisman)

Early in 1958 Rob Rennie, a young motor racing fan, visited the Walker workshops. Now, sixty years later, Rob recalls the day that has lived long in his memory.

> 'Just before the Argentine race, a friend of mine offered me the chance to visit the Rob Walker workshops at Pippbrook. So, on the 8th January 1958, which was a grey wet day as I remember, I was driven to Dorking by family friend Lieutenant Commander Robert Walsh the then prospective Liberal candidate for Mole Valley. We arrived and entered the racing workshop where the Cooper, stripped of its bodywork, was being worked on by Alf Francis no less. I chatted briefly to Alf about the car's race preparation and he explained he was under a tight schedule as the car needed to be air freighted to Buenos Aires the following week. It was a great privilege to meet Alf and see him at work. Little did I appreciate as an impressionable lad of just 15 that 1958 would see the R R C Walker Racing Team emerge onto the Grand Prix stage in such dramatic fashion.'

Indeed, 1958 proved to be the start of the team's golden decade, which saw Rob Walker's blue and white cars taking the chequered flag at world championship races around the world. These achievements began in Argentina at only the team's third overseas grand prix.

Race Report: The 1958 Argentine Grand Prix

The 1958 Argentine Grand Prix was held in Buenos Aires and was the opening round of the Formula One season. The race was run over 80 laps of the four-kilometre circuit, a total distance of 313 kilometres (194 miles). The British teams Vanwall and BRM (with both of whom Stirling was contracted to drive) were not prepared for the race due to problems converting their cars from methanol to 'pump petrol'. Vanwall gave Stirling permission to drive a Cooper T43 entered by Rob Walker. Compared to the other, more powerful and much larger cars on the grid, the tiny Cooper with its underpowered 1.9 litre engine was considered a bit of a joke by the other teams.

Due to the extremely hot conditions, the race distance was shortened from 400 kilometres to 313. This led the Walker team to devise a cunning but risky strategy to complete the race without stopping for new tyres. Alf Francis and Tim Wall, a second mechanic from the Walker team, openly discussed how much time they would lose by having to make a pit stop for new tyres, as there was no chance of Moss competing the race on one set of tyres. Or was there?

A Maserati 250F driven by privateer Jean Behra powered off the grid to an early lead. Disaster seemed to have struck Moss on lap 4 when the Cooper's clutch broke, leaving the gearbox jammed in second gear. Soon after a stone, thrown up from the track, lodged itself into the car's transmission mechanism. This incredible stroke of luck enabled Moss to engage the rest of his gears for the remainder of the race.

Mike Hawthorn's Ferrari Dino 246 soon took the lead, but he was passed by his team-mate Juan Manuel Fangio on lap ten. But as the heavier Italian cars stopped for new tyres, Moss, in his much lighter Cooper, drove his way into second position.

Rob Walker's 1957 Cooper Climax T43 still going strong at the Goodwood Festival of Speed.

In a successful ploy to fool the other teams that they were about to make a pit stop, the Walker team busied themselves preparing new tyres for Moss. However, by the end of the pitstops the little Cooper had moved into the lead, with the Italian Musso and Hawthorn behind. A misfire slowed Fangio and a spin delayed Behra. By lap 70 the other teams had realised that Moss was staying out and was not stopping for new tyres.

Musso and Hawthorn were ordered to pick up their pace in an effort to catch Moss, whose tyres were now beginning to disintegrate. Moss however, nursed his car to the chequered flag and crossed the line just 2.7 seconds ahead of Musso and Hawthorn. The first Maserati to finish was

A rear tyre from the Cooper showing that three of the five canvas layers had worn away.

Fangio in fourth, followed by Behra, who was two laps down in fifth. Examination of Moss' tyres after the race revealed that they had worn through three of their five canvas layers and probably would have lasted just one more lap!

It was an historic race on four counts. It was the first post war win for a rear-engine racing car; the first win by a Cooper chassis; the first win for a privateer team; and, most importantly, it was the Rob Walker Team's first Formula One Grand Prix win. The nimble little Cooper's win was a shock to the establishment and it sounded the death knell for the front-engine racing car.

Winning Driver Profile: Stirling Moss

Born on 17th September 1929, Sir Stirling Moss OBE, became known as 'Mr Motor Racing' and was one of the all-time great drivers. He turned professional at the age of 18 and was a true all-rounder. Apart from driving for Rob Walker he also drove for Aston Martin, Ferrari, Maserati, Mercedes-Benz, Jaguar and Vanwall. His successes were not all in Formula One: he raced at Le Mans and won the Mille Miglia 1,000-mile road race in a Mercedes-Benz 300 SLR.

Moss finished runner-up in the Formula One Drivers' World Championship four times, coming closest to winning in 1958 when he lost by half a point to another Englishman, Mike Hawthorn. During his racing career, he drove in 375 competitive races and, amazingly, won 212 of them.

From 1958 to 1962 Moss drove in over 90 races for Rob Walker and won 46 of them. He was lucky to survive a bad accident at Spa in 1960, which ruled him out for most of that season. He returned in 1961 and produced two of his greatest races, even though his Lotus 18 was outclassed by the stunning Ferrari 156 'shark-nose'. The first win came in Argentina; the second was in Germany. It was, however, his last full racing season.

Moss was racing at Goodwood on Easter Monday 23rd April 1962 when, for unknown reasons (possibly some kind of mechanical failure), his Formula 1 BRP Lotus veered out of control and smashed into a grass bank. Moss was gravely injured and in a coma for a month.

He attempted a comeback a year later when, again at Goodwood, he took part in a private test session. The test proved that he could still produce competitive lap times but his natural reactions to the car had gone. The career of one of the greatest racing drivers was over.

To put it simply, Moss excelled in everything he drove. A measure of Ferrari's esteem for him can be seen in the arrangement the team was willing to make to secure his services. Shortly before his crash, Moss had told the Ferrari team boss, Enzo Ferrari, that he would be happy to drive for him only if Rob Walker ran the team, to which Ferrari agreed. If Moss had not had his Goodwood accident we would have seen a Pippbrook-prepared Ferrari, painted in Rob Walker's blue and white, competing on the world's race circuits.

Winning Car Specifications: Cooper T43 Formula 2

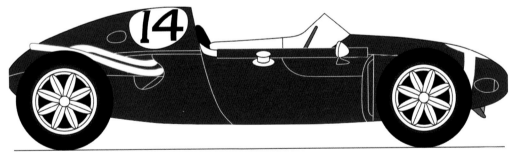

Constructor: Cooper Cars, Surbiton, Surrey
Year: 1958
Engine: Coventry-Climax FPF
Capacity: 1475cc
Power: 190 bhp (139.84 kw) at 6500 rpm
Weight: 1000 lbs (454 kg)
Wheelbase: 104 ins (2,642 mm)

By the time the teams gathered together in the South of France for the Monaco Grand Prix, Moss had returned to Vanwall and Maurice Trintignant had taken over the Cooper. Ferrari's reputation was dented once again as the Walker team pushed them into second place at the season's most prestigious race. Trintignant's victory (his first Formula One) proved that the Argentinian win was not a flash in the pan. Trintignant also finished third at the German Grand Prix at the Nürburgring.

Other Walker Formula One successes in 1958 were non-title wins for Moss at the Caen and Melbourne Grands Prix. There were also F2 wins for Moss at Brands Hatch and Trintignant at Pau, Caen and Clermont-Ferrand. All in all it was quite a season for the Dorking-based team.

1959 Season

Back at Pippbrook the team experienced year-long gearbox problems. However, Moss won in Portugal and at the Italian Grand Prix at Monza, and went into the last race, the United States Grand Prix at Sebring, as a title contender. He needed to win the race and record the fastest lap, which was worth an extra championship point in those days. Unfortunately, he was forced to retire early and finished the World Championship in third place, behind Tony Brooks and Jack Brabham, who won his first of three titles that year. Non-championship wins at Goodwood and Oulton Park provided some consolation.

Alf Francis, Tim Wall and John Chisman, watched by Rob, install the BRM engine into a Cooper chassis at the Pippbrook workshop in 1959. (Robbie Walker)

Chapter 4

1960s Triumph & Tragedy

Motor racing in the 1950s and 60s was a highly dangerous occupation; safety precautions were poor or non-existent and it was not uncommon for two or three drivers to be killed in a season. Tragedy would strike the Walker Team more than once in the same year.

The Racing Family

The motor racing community was tight-knit, with a great sense of camaraderie and friendship. Teams would organise fishing trips (see above) and run a sweepstake on which team would arrive first at the circuit for the next race. On the track drivers and teams would assist one another with the loan of tools and spare parts. On one occasion Tony Cleverly even welded a fuel tank to assist the Ferrari team. Rob's wife Betty was part of that family; she became an essential part of the team, keeping lap times from the pit wall.

Rob Walker looks on as Moss and John Chisman discuss the Cooper. (Jim Chisman)

1960 Season

Rob chose to concentrate exclusively on Moss for the 1960 season. The new Lotus 18, the latest creation from legendary car designer Colin Chapman, showed great potential. Moss won the Monaco Grand Prix, the team's first World Championship win, and looked to be the driver to beat for the title. But yet again it was not to be his year.

During the Belgian Grand Prix at Spa a serious crash, caused by a broken drive shaft, put him out of action for two months. The race also saw the tragic deaths of two British drivers, Chris Bristow and Alan Stacey. Moss came back to win the United States Grand Prix at Riverside and, for the second successive year, finished the championship in third place. Away from Formula

A model of the 1960 Walker Formula 2 Porsche from the Dorking Museum collection. (Royston Williamson)

One, Stirling drove the Walker team's new Formula 2 Porsche at Syracuse in Sicily, but failed to finish. However, he did win the Aintree 200 F2 race in the Porsche and collected two second place finishes during the season at Silverstone and Goodwood. And he drove Rob's beautiful Ferrari 250 SWB to win the 1960 Tourist Trophy sports car race at Goodwood.

1961 Season

Unable to buy a new Lotus 21 for the 1961 Formula One season, the team was forced to work on the outdated Lotus 18. Moss managed to achieve pole position for the first race of the season at Monaco, with the Ferrari of Ritchie Ginther and Jim Clark's new Lotus 21 alongside. Phil Hill and Wolfgang von Trips drove the two remaining Ferraris. Due to the extremely hot conditions on race day, the team removed the side-panels on Moss's car to aid cooling. Just before the start a crack was noticed on one of the car's frame tubes, which Alf Francis corrected

Stirling Moss (number 20) on pole position at the start of the 1961 Monaco Grand Prix.

on the grid using a welding torch! During the race, in a sustained effort to harass Moss into a mistake, the three Ferrari drivers repeatedly swapped positions. This spurred Moss to drive even harder and he took the chequered flag after 100 laps and 2¾ hours of virtuoso driving to claim his third Monaco Grand Prix, a record at that time. Phil Hill later described his efforts to catch Moss during the race as being like 'a horse chasing a greyhound around a living room'.

Moss was also victorious at the German Grand Prix in terribly wet conditions around the mighty Nürburgring in front of a 100,000-strong crowd. It was one of his finest races. But he finished third in the championship yet again, in what would be his last full racing season.

Stirling Moss in the pits during practice for the 1961 German Grand Prix. Moss won the race in heavy rain.

His Pippbrook team accomplished a unique motorsport first in 1961, when Walker entered the Ferguson P99 Climax in the non-world championship Oulton Park Gold Cup. With Moss at the wheel it became the first, and probably only, four-wheel drive car ever to win a Formula One race. Moss also drove Rob's Ferrari 250 SWB sports car to win the 1961 Goodwood Tourist Trophy for the second successive year.

Rob's Ferrari 250 SWB shines in the sun at Goodwood, while Alf Francis reads the paper. (Rob Rennie)

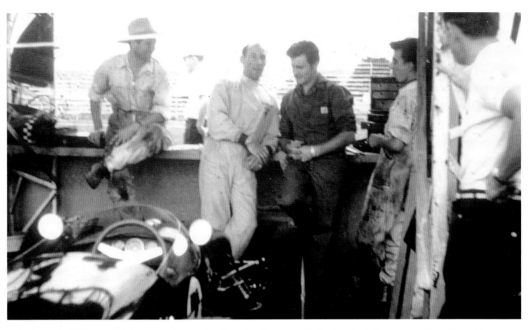

It's the early 1960s, and Stirling Moss is seen chatting with his mechanics in the pits before a race. (Tony Cleverly)

Swedish driver Jo Bonnier drove a Cooper-Climax for The Walker team during the 1963 season. He finished in eleventh place in the drivers' World Championship that year. (Rob Rennie)

Growing the Business

As Walker's business grew, the Pippbrook Garage began to offer vehicle servicing and MOT testing to the public. He later opened a Ford car dealership and showroom. In 1968 it was possible to buy an 'immaculate' 1967 Ford Corsair two-door V4 de-luxe saloon in blue, with a heater, washers, reversing light and wing mirrors - all for £665!

Keen to keep in touch with his customers, Rob sent out regular issues of 'The Pippbrook Post', a monthly newsletter which contained sales news and motoring tips. He also ran social events, including car treasure hunts and an Italian evening at Dorking Halls to launch the new Ford Capri. The newsletter's Children's Corner contained paintings and road safety competitions and he sold a comic, 'The Wonder Weekly', at the garage for sixpence. The garage also had its own ladies' netball team, The Pippbrook Tigers. The latest news from the racing team, including car and driver details and race results, were also reported in 'The Pippbrook Post'.

The Walker-Climax

Back in 1959 Rob had begun a project to produce his own Formula One car, 'The Walker-Climax'. Alf Francis, Rob's chief mechanic, designed the car, which was based on a Cooper. The intention was to improve upon and develop the proven factory car, but progress was slow and the car was not finally tested until 1961, by which time it was out of date. It was stored un-raced for many years but has been rebuilt and is now driven at historic meetings.

The fully restored Walker Climax at the 2010 Goodwood Revival. (Rob Rennie)

PIPPBROOK POST

Number 7, August 1968

Victory smiles from Rob Walker and his driver Jo Siffert, pictured at Brands Hatch, where the Rob Walker team carried off the British Grand Prix prize, amid congratulations from the whole motoring world. Full report on our inside pages.

WITH THE COMPLIMENTS OF ROB WALKER, PIPPBROOK GARAGES, DORKING

The cover of the Pippbrook Post from August 1968. Apart from news of the racing team, the 'Post' also featured car servicing advice, social events and children's competitions. (Dorking Museum)

Graham Hill racing the Walker Ferguson P99 4 wheel drive car at Lakeside, New Zealand during the International Gold Star meeting in February 1963. (Photograph reproduced with permission of the Briar Thomas Collection)

Jo Siffert behind the wheel of the 3-Litre Cooper-Maserati during a test session at Modena, Italy. (Tony Cleverly)

1962 Season - A Dark Year

1961 proved a rewarding year but 1962 would bring heartbreak and tragedy to Pippbrook. Following Stirling Moss's career-ending accident at Goodwood, Rob brought Maurice Trintignant back into the Formula One team for the 1962 season. He was driving the new Lotus 24, but was not able to repeat his past glories.

The team also suffered two tragic incidents during the season involving young rising stars. In February the Mexican driver Ricardo Rodriguez was killed in a 120-mph accident while practising for his home Grand Prix in Mexico City; he was just nineteen years old. In December of the same year Gary Hocking was practising for the Natal Grand Prix in South Africa when he was killed.

Hocking was born in Wales but grew up in Southern Rhodesia. He had enjoyed a successful career on two wheels before he switched to car racing. Deeply affected by the death of a friend at the 1962 Isle of Man TT, he had concluded that motorcycle racing had become too dangerous and decided that a car racing career would be safer. He was 25 years old when he died. Rodriguez and Hocking were the first (and thankfully the last) drivers to die at the wheel of his cars and Rob, who was deeply shocked, considered giving up racing altogether.

1963 Season

For the following three F1 seasons the aristocratic Swede Jo Bonnier drove for the Walker Formula One team. Driving a Cooper throughout 1963, he was placed eleventh in the drivers' world championship. He achieved a total of nine top ten finishes at Monaco, Belgium, Holland, France, Germany, Italy, USA, Mexico and South Africa.

In 1963 Alf Francis left Dorking, but would return some years later to maintain Rob's classic car collection. Tony Cleverly became the head mechanic. On the business front, the car service and repair company Tutts began renting the front and middle workshop buildings from Rob Walker.

1964 Season

The 1964 Formula One season was not a great success. After a fifth place at Monaco driving a Cooper, Bonnier drove a Brabham for the rest of the season. Three mid place finishes and four retirements produced just three points. But towards the end of the year Swiss driver Jo Siffert raced in two Grand Prix for the Rob Walker Team, finishing in third place in the USA.

Working at Pippbrook

Rob continued to live in Nunney, near Frome in Somerset, with his wife and two children. He made his regular journeys to Dorking in a range of high powered sports cars, including a white Mercedes-Benz 300SL 'gull-wing'. Rob's secretary at Pippbrook was Liz Piper. She became an essential part of the team and handled all the racing administration for many years.

Eric Mansfield, who worked at Pippbrook as a panel beater, recalls the team's mechanics (and sometimes drivers) test driving cars from the racing shop along the A24 dual carriageway to the Burford Bridge roundabout and back. These tests were often followed by a visit to the workshops by the police after local residents called them to report loud engine noises. On arrival at Pippbrook they were offered a cup of tea and biscuits to smooth things over.

PIPPBROOK GARAGES LTD

DIRECTORS: R. R. C. WALKER · S. R. JOLLIFFE (MANAGING)   MAIN *Ford* DEALER   TELEPHONE : 3891 — 2 — 3 — 4

London Road
DORKING

Rob Walker's Pippbrook Garage, Ford dealership and Esso petrol station in 1965. Copyright The Francis Frith Collection.

In 1968 Eric built a set of aluminium end plates for the rear wing of the team's Lotus 49 and devised an ingenious way to test their aerodynamic shape. He constructed a wooden pattern and then waded into the Pipp Brook, a stream which ran alongside the racing shop. Placing the pattern into the flowing water Eric studied the aerodynamic performance. The technique worked, the high rear wing on the Walker Lotus proved strong and effective.

1965 Season

In 1965 Rob acquired a second BRM-powered Brabham to run a two-car Formula One team; the popular Siffert drove the second car alongside Bonnier. Siffert was one of nature's gentlemen and the two became lifelong friends.

1965 was quite a year on the Grand Prix front. There was a remarkable win by Siffert in the non-championship Mediterranean Grand Prix at Enna in Sicily. The race developed into a nose-to-tail struggle between Siffert and the double world-champion Jim Clark, with Siffert crossing the line first. Bonnier retired five times and finished five times, but in low positions. Siffert had eight finishes with two retirements, but even so he finished twelfth in the world championship.

1966-1967 Seasons

Jo Bonnier left the Walker team in 1966 and was later killed while driving in the 1972 Le Mans 24-hour race. Rob returned to a single car line up, with Siffert driving a 3-Litre Cooper-Maserati. 1966 was not a good year for the team however, with a string of disappointing retirements and just one completed race, a fourth place in the USA. The cost of running a Formula One team was beginning to escalate, and in 1967 stockbroker and entrepreneur Jack Durlacher joined the team, bringing with him additional financial backing. The Walker team did not make a podium finish during the season, with a best placed fourth in France and the USA.

1968 Season - A Last Hurrah

Siffert remained with Walker for the 1968 Formula One season, driving the now ageing Cooper into seventh place at the first race of the season in South Africa. For the rest of the 1968 season he would drive the new Lotus 49.

A devastating fire at Pippbrook

On Saturday 16th March 1968 Rob was at Brands Hatch when he received a distressing phone call from his manager at Pippbrook Garage, Stan Jolliffe. A serious fire had broken out at the London Road racing shop.

A frightening sight as fire tears through the Walker team workshops in London Road. (Jim Chisman)

The day before Siffert, who was practising for the non-championship Race of Champions at Brands Hatch in the Lotus 49B R4, had hit a damp patch of track following a rain shower and crashed. The car, in which Jim Clark won the 1968 South African Grand Prix in January, had been returned to Pippbrook for repairs. Whilst working on it a spark from a mechanic's electric drill had ignited a devastating fire, which destroyed the car, a Cooper-Maserati, a Type 52 Bugatti, and two new Ford DFV engines. Also lost in the fire were some of Rob's most treasured possessions from 30 years of racing, including a tyre from Stirling's 1958 Argentina Grand Prix win and a scrapbook containing newspaper clippings and photos from all the races he drove in. Another casualty of the fire was Rob's beautifully restored 1927 Delage, which someone thoughtfully moved to another location before Rob saw it.

The fire spread so quickly and was so fierce that Tony Cleverly only escaped by jumping out of the window into the Pipp Brook. Fortunately, no one was seriously injured and the other buildings on the site were not damaged, but the racing shop was completely gutted. With his cars destroyed, Rob faced the closure of his racing team, but with help from his brother-in-law he managed to rebuild. An ex-Jim Clark Tasman Lotus 49 was acquired from Lotus boss Colin Chapman for Siffert to drive, so the team did not miss a race. A new car (a Lotus 49B R7) was delivered in time for the British Grand Prix which was partly prepared at Milton Motors Garage in the town. The garage had just been bought by Woolworths to enlarge their store but before construction work began they loaned the premises to Walker. Soon after the team relocated down the A24 to Rob's Beare Green Garage and did not return to Pippbrook.

Race Report: 1968 British Grand Prix

The seventh round of the 1968 Formula One season was the British Grand Prix, run over 80 laps on Sunday 20th July at Brands Hatch in Kent.

Graham Hill started on pole (winning 100 bottles of champagne for his efforts) ahead of Lotus team-mate Jackie Oliver, with Chris Amon's Ferrari the third car to complete the front row. On the second row were Siffert and Jochen Rindt, ahead of Dan Gurney, Jackie Stewart and Jack Brabham. Next were John Surtees, Bruce McLaren and the reigning World Champion Denny Hulme, who qualified eleventh. Amon's Ferrari team-mate Jacky Ickx was back in twelfth place and Pedro Rodriquez thirteenth in a BRM. The Walker team arrived late at the track and missed the first three quarters of an hour of practice.

Tony Cleverly cautiously manoeuvres Jo Siffert's Lotus 49 through the Brands Hatch paddock in 1968. It is a world away from the high-security , no-access paddocks of modern grand prix race tracks. (Tony Cleverly)

Rain showers earlier in the day had cleared by the time the field of 20 cars were marshalled to their grid positions. As the Union Jack dropped to start the race (no red lights in 1968!) the Cooper-BRM of Vic Elford failed to turn over, along with Dan Gurney's Eagle, and both cars were out. The rest of the field managed to avoid any contact and thundered towards the first corner, led by Oliver then Hill, Siffert, Amon, Stewart and Surtees.

Championship leader Hill took the lead on lap three after his team-mate Oliver let him pass. Surtees moved up to fifth after overtaking Stewart on the thirteenth lap. A rear suspension failure on lap 27 forced Hill's Lotus into the pits and retirement from the race, much to the disappointment of the largely home crowd.

OFFICIAL PROGRAMME 2s 6d

a spectacle of *speed & sound*

BRITISH GRAND PRIX

world championship race sponsored by the DAILY MAIL

BRANDS HATCH 20th JULY 1968

As the remaining cars began to thin out, Siffert and Amon chased Oliver in the number two works Lotus. Behind them Surtees was holding on to fourth, followed by Stewart and Ickx, who had passed Hulme. Starting next to each other on the grid, the Belgian and the Kiwi had carved through the field, overtaking McLaren, Rindt and Rodriguez.

The two passed Stewart on lap 32, but soon afterwards Ickx made a mistake, allowing Hulme to overtake. The two swapped places once again before the end of the race. By lap 40 Oliver, who had passed Siffert, was ten seconds ahead of Amon. Ickx had passed Surtees' badly-handling Honda, which had lost its rear wing. Siffert passed Amon to move into second place on lap 44, and soon afterwards took the lead as Oliver retired with a wheel problem.

Amon, determined to keep the pressure on Siffert, started to increase his lap times, but a fault with a rear tyre meant he could not keep up with the Lotus. During the closing laps Stewart, who was now suffering considerable pain from a recent wrist injury, closed right up to the back of Surtees' Honda, but was unable to find a way to pass. On lap 56 a leaking fuel pipe ignited on Rindt's Braham, leading to a fiery exit for the Austrian.

Just four seconds separated Amon from Siffert as they crossed the finish line. It was Siffert's first Grand Prix win and the first by a Swiss driver. A lap down in third place was Ickx, and then came Hulme, Surtees and Stewart. The win was a very popular one with the knowledgeable Brands Hatch crowd, who cheered and applauded as Siffert, Rob Walker and the winning car completed a lap of honour on the back of a parade truck. This was the ninth and last victory by the Rob Walker Racing Team and almost certainly the last win by a truly private entrant.

A 1968 magazine advert for Rob Walker's Lotus dealership in Warminster.

Winning Driver Profile: Jo Siffert

Joseph (Seppi) Siffert was born on the 7th July 1936. His family ran a small dairy business in Fribourg, Switzerland. In July 1948 his father took him to his first motor race, the Grand Prix of Europe at Bremgarten near Bern. At first sight of a grand prix car at full speed little Seppi ran back to his father shouting, 'He's gone. Papa, he was going very fast!' From that moment Siffert, just like his future boss Rob Walker, was hooked on motor racing. During that weekend two drivers were killed, a grave forewarning to the young Siffert of the dangers of motor racing.

Siffert started to drive at the age of eleven on his father's farm; his family were astonished at how well he drove without having been taught. After passing his driving test in 1954 he took an apprenticeship as a coachbuilder. Two years of National Service followed, when he worked as a mechanic.

Siffert began his racing career on two wheels; in 1959 he won the Swiss 350cc motorcycle championship. Switching to cars he moved to F1 in 1962, driving his own Lotus-Climax. He joined Rob Walker in 1964 and finished third in his first F1 race for the team at the USA Grand Prix.

Like most of his contemporaries Siffert not only competed in Formula One but also in other categories, including Formula Two, CanAm and sports cars. In 1966 and 1967 he achieved class wins at Le Mans and in 1968 won the Daytona 24 Hours race.

By the end of the 1971 season Siffert had driven in 40 races and had won the Dutch Grand Prix. He was unsure about entering the last race of the year which was planned to celebrate Jackie Stewart's winning the 1971 F1 World Drivers' Championship. The race took place on 24th October at Brands Hatch, the scene of Siffert's memorable win three years earlier. On lap 16 the rear suspension on his BRM, which had been damaged earlier in the race, broke suddenly. Out of control along the fast Pilgrims Drop straight, the car hit a bank, turned over and burst into flames. Siffert was killed instantly.

Rob Walker was devastated by the news. Siffert's funeral in Fribourg was attended by 50,000 people. A procession around the town was headed by a Gulf Porsche 917 that Jo had raced at Le Mans. During his twelve-year career Siffert had competed in over 190 motorsport events. A professional racing driver who loved motorsport, he paid the ultimate price.

Winning Car Specifications: Lotus 49B R7

Constructor: Lotus Cars, Hethel, Norfolk

Class: Formula 1

Engine: 90 degrees V8 Ford-Cosworth DFV

Capacity: 2,998 cc

Power: 400 bhp (298.28 kw) at 9,000 rpm

Weight: 1,105 lbs (501 kg)

Wheelbase: 95.0 ins (2,413 mm)

Following the Brands Hatch win, the remainder of the 1968 season was an anti-climax for the team with three consecutive non-finishes. However, Siffert drove to fifth place in the United States and sixth in Mexico and ended the year in seventh place in the drivers' championship with 12 points.

Jo Siffert's Lotus 49 is refuelled before the start of the 1968 United States Grand Prix at Watkins Glen. (Tony Cleverly)

The Walker team and their Lotus 49 in the pits at Watkins Glen, USA in 1968.(Tony Cleverly)

1969 Season

Positive results kept coming in 1969, with Siffert finishing fourth in South Africa, third in Monaco, second in Holland and fifth in Germany. He ended the year in ninth place in the drivers' championship with a total of 15 points. Siffert left the team at the end of the season and moved to Brabham.

During their four years together Rob Walker and Jo Siffert had formed a strong friendship, and Rob would follow the rest of Siffert's career with great interest. Siffert's departure signalled the end of the team's 'golden decade' and the beginning of the end for the team itself.

A quiet corner in the Pippbrook racing shop before the fire. An Austin 7, surrounded by racing tyres, waits its turn for some mechanical attention. (Robbie Walker)

The Phoenix Rises

Of all the cars destroyed in the Pippbrook fire the 1927 Richard Seaman Delage was the hardest for Rob to take, particularly as John Chisman's beautiful restoration had only been completed in 1964.

Fire damage was extensive. The whole of the body had gone, the car's iron girder frame had melted and was sagging to the ground. The engine blower covers had also melted, the engine valves were bent, the tyres were burnt away and the wheels were beyond repair. Rob judged the car to be a complete write-off.

About a month after the fire John Chisman speculatively tried to turn the engine with the rusty starting handle and found to his amazement that the engine appeared to be free. On closer scrutiny John also found the engine block and sump were relatively undamaged. Was there a chance of a second restoration? A full inspection was carried out, after which the decision was made to give this unique car another chance.

Smoke rises around the burnt out Delage in the sad remains of the Pippbrook racing shop on 16th March 1968. (Jim Chisman)

The daunting job of restoration began with the manufacturing of new cam covers and brake drums. For the chassis two pieces of wood between the two front dumb irons, which strengthen the chassis and reduce flexing, were needed. Local undertakers Sherlocks volunteered to make new ones out of the best oak coffin wood.

A fire damaged photo of the Delage on the Pippbrook Garage forecourt during its first restoration by John Chisman. (Jim Chisman)

The gearbox was damaged, but serviced back to its original condition. Felt for all the oil seals was bought from a local saddle maker and made up by Jim Chisman. There were some remarkable finds during the restoration. A replacement for the car's Bosch magneto was found in the company's museum in Switzerland. The radiator was remade by the same man who built the original back in 1930s.

The Delage sits gleaming in the London Road yard after its two year restoration by John Chisman. (Jim Chisman)

A new body was built by Wakefields of Byfleet by two panel beaters who worked on the same car during its Brooklands days. The finishing touch, a replacement front badge, came from the Delage Owners' Club.

The restored Delage made its first appearance at a motor show in December 1970. When the engine was fired up the noise of the engine cleared the exhibition hall. The Phoenix had well and truly risen; the Delage was back!

Chapter 5

1970s The Last Lap

O n 9th January 1970 the Dorking Advertiser reported that Rob Walker had announced his intention to sell the Pippbrook Garage. As all his mechanics lived in the Dorking area he would continue to base his racing team at his workshops in Beare Green. The workshop fire two years previously had cost him a great deal of money and he needed to sell the Pippbrook workshops.

1970 Season

Formula One running costs were spiralling and in 1970 Rob negotiated his first major sponsorship deal with the Brooke Bond Oxo group. This enabled him to hire the double ex-world champion, Graham Hill, to drive the Lotus 49.

Graham Hill, on his way to 5th place at the 1970 Race of Champions at Brands Hatch. (Insert) Hill makes a rather shifty look to camera. (both photos Stewart Booth)

Left to right, two times Formula One World Champion Graham Hill, Norman Bingham marketing director for Brooke Bond Oxo and Rob Walker standing in front of the team's transporter. (Robbie Walker)

Although Hill was recovering from severe leg injuries sustained at the United States Grand Prix the previous year, he managed to finish in sixth place in the South African Grand Prix, fifth in the non-championship Race of Champions at Brands Hatch, and fourth in the Spanish Grand Prix. But after competing in eleven races, he ended the year in a disappointing thirteenth place in the drivers' championship with just seven points. He left at the end of the season to join the Brabham Team, and Rob was left with the difficult decision of whether or not to continue to run his team from Dorking.

1971 Season-Goodbye to Dorking

Although he was concerned about the future of his employees in Dorking, Rob decided to join forces with his old friend, John Surtees (left), for the 1971 season. Surtees, who is the only man to have won the Formula One world championship and to have been crowned World Motorbike Champion, was also facing financial difficulties with his F1 racing team. So, taking his Brooke Bond Oxo sponsorship with him, Rob merged his team with Surtees', which was based in Edenbridge, Kent.

Mike Hailwood's Surtees TS9 during practice at Brands Hatch for the 1971 Jackie Stewart World Championship Victory Race. Hailwood was in fifth place when the race was stopped following Jo Siffert's fatal accident. (Stewart Booth)

Built after the 1968 fire, this view of the Walker restoration workshop was taken in 1970s. On the right is Rob's 1936 Delahaye 135 Course, next to a Ferrari Dino 196S, with a Bugatti Type 52 in front. Laid out on the floor are engine parts from the Delage which is waiting rebuilding. (Jim Chisman)

The racing team would no longer be based in Dorking. However, Walker opened a new workshop building in London Road to service his classic car collection. Alf Francis joined John Chisman there. Walker also took it upon himself to try to find employment for the other team members who had served him so well over the years.

During his 17-year career with the Rob Walker Team Tony Cleverly travelled the world and witnessed some of the greatest races in Grand Prix history. Looking back, he recalls his time working alongside Rob Walker, the drivers and his teammates with huge affection: "It was great every day and I would do it all again if I could".

1972-1973 Seasons

The Walker-Surtees partnership lasted another two seasons, but Rob was never again to see one of his drivers win a Formula One race. Rob's old friend Mike 'The Bike' Hailwood (right) had switched from two wheels to four and was driving for the Surtees team in 1972. Other drivers who raced for the team during this period included Tim Schenken, Carlos Pace and Rolf Stommelen.

Mike Hailwood (21) in the Walker/Surtees leads François Cevert's Tyrrell during the 1972 British Grand Prix at Brands Hatch. Both cars retired from the race, which was won by the Brazilian Emerson Fittipaldi. (Stewart Booth)

Mike Hailwood's gleaming 1973 TS14 at Brooklands Mercedes Benz World for an exhibition celebrating the life and achievements of John Surtees, who died in 2017.

1974 Season

The Brooke Bond Oxo sponsorship ended in 1973. Rob left Surtees and followed Hailwood to the Yardley McLaren team for the 1974 season. Walker lost another friend when Mike and his young daughter were killed in a road traffic accident in 1981.

1975 Season

In 1975 the Rob Walker Racing Team made a brief reappearance when Rob teamed up with the former double British Formula Three Champion, Harry Stiller. Together they ran an old Hesketh car for the future Formula One world champion, Australian Alan Jones. Rob also assisted the Hesketh and Embassy-Hill teams with timekeeping. But his involvement in motor racing was coming to an end.

Rob Walker had been working in motor racing management for over thirty years, but the new world of wheeler-dealing with company sponsors was not his style and he would not have considered it to be the way that a gentleman should race. It was time to move on. But his new career would keep him close to the sport that he had loved all his life.

The Chequered Flag

After retirement from racing management, Rob put his experience to good use. He became a motorsport journalist for the American Road & Track magazine. (He had been writing race reports for Road & Track and other racing publications, including Motorsport magazine, for some years before his retirement.) He maintained his interest and love of motorsport right up until his death in 2002 from pneumonia, which he caught after a soaking playing golf. He was 84 years old.

Rob Walker was a kind and generous man who became a motor racing institution. He was held in great affection and respected by everyone in the sport, and by all who met him. The occupation on his passport simply read 'gentleman' and above all that is what he was.

Rob Walker at the wheel of his beloved Delahaye at the Goodwood Revival meeting. (Robbie Walker)

Pippbrook Garage in 2018. The present building is functional, but hasn't the character of its predecessor.

Pippbrook Today

Since the Rob Walker days, the Pippbrook Garage has been rebuilt several times and sadly no trace of the original Art-Deco building survives. A busy Esso petrol station is still operating on the site, but the showroom and service workshops have long gone.

During the 1970s Tutts bought the London Road entire site, but another fire in 1984 destroyed the remaining original buildings, after which new workshops were constructed. These were demolished following Tutts' relocation to workshops in Curtis Road in 2010. The site was completely cleared in 2011, when construction work began on the development of town houses, known appropriately as Tutts' Close.

Tutts Close in 2018.

And so today there is no evidence or permanent reminder on the London Road site of its historic racing past. But many of Rob Walker's racing cars have been preserved in excellent condition and are displayed in museums or housed in private collections around the world. Some are still even raced at historic meetings, such as the Goodwood Revival. These beautiful cars, now worth many hundreds of thousands of pounds, are treasured by their owners and provide an enduring, and a glorious sounding, reminder of Rob Walker's part in motor racing history.

A selection of Rob Walker cars that are raced and exhibited at historic race meetings around the world. (top to bottom) Lotus 18, Cooper Climax T43, Lotus 49, and the Ferguson P99a at the Goodwood Revival, and a Surtees ST9B at Mallory Park.

The Rob Walker Centenary Festival
Sunday 21st October 2018

To tie in with the Dorking Museum's Rob Walker Exhibition, an historic parade of ex-Walker racing cars around Dorking town centre is being planned by the Dorking Town Partnership. As this book nears completion these plans are at a very advanced stage with agreement from the owners of the following nine cars to take part:

1958 Argentine Grand Prix winning CooperT43 Climax

1958 Monaco Grand Prix winning Cooper T43 Climax

1960 Tourist Trophy winning Ferrari 250SWB

1961 Monaco Grand Prix winning Lotus 18 Climax

1961 Oulton Park Gold Cup winning Ferguson P99FWD Climax

1961 Tourist Trophy winning Ferrari 250SWB

1936 Delahaye 135S raced by Rob Walker

1927 Delage S15 Grand Prix - Brooklands Museum (static)

1972 Surtees TS14B DFV - as raced by Mike Hailwood /Carlos Pace

This event will be the culmination of over two years planning and was first suggested by Rob Rennie, who visited the Walker team workshops as a teenager back in 1958.

A painting sketch by the renowned motor racing artist Michael Turner. It shows the planned grid formation in Dorking High Street during the Rob Walker Centenary Festival parade around the town centre.

Appendix 1

The Winning Formula

While based in Dorking between 1949 and 1968 the Rob Walker Team won 9 Formula One World Championship Grand Prix, including three wins around the tight streets of Monaco.

Race	Driver	Car
1958 Argentina	Stirling Moss	Cooper Climax T45
1958 Monaco	Maurice Trintignant	Cooper Climax T45
1959 Portugal	Stirling Moss	Cooper Climax T51
1959 Italy	Stirling Moss	Cooper Climax T51
1960 Monaco	Stirling Moss	Lotus 18
1960 United States	Stirling Moss	Lotus 18
1961 Monaco	Stirling Moss	Lotus 18
1961 Germany	Stirling Moss	Lotus 18
1968 Britain	Jo Siffert	Lotus 49

Out of a total of 124 Formula One race starts the team also achieved 10 pole positions and 9 fastest laps. During this time Rob Walker entered racing cars from the following constructors: Connaught, Cooper, Lotus, Ferguson and Brabham.

Non-championship races

The following pages list the team's non-championship race entries between 1949 and 1970.

Note:
Races between 1950 and 1952 were often mixed formula (Formula 1 and 2).

Non-championship races	Date	Driver
1949 British Empire Trophy	26/05/1949	Guy Jason-Henry
		Tony Rolt
1949 Le Mans 24 Hours	25/06/1949	Guy Jason-Henry
1949 French Grand Prix	07/08/1949	Guy Jason-Henry
		Tony Rolt
1950 British Empire Trophy	15/06/1950	John Rowley
1950 Jersey F1	13/07/1950	Tony Rolt
1950 International Trophy	26/08/1950	Tony Rolt
1951 International Trophy	05/05/1951	Tony Rolt
1951 Ulster Trophy	02/06/1951	Peter Walker
1951 Goodwood F1	29/09/1951	Tony Rolt
1952 Goodwood F1	14/04/1952	Tony Rolt
1953 Rouen Grand Prix	28/06/1953	Stirling Moss
1954 Goodwood F1	19/04/1954	Tony Rolt
1954 International Trophy	15/05/1954	Tony Rolt
1954 Crystal Palace F1	19/06/1954	Peter Collins
1954 Crystal Palace F1	02/08/1954	Tony Rolt
1954 Oulton Park Gold Cup	07/08/1954	John Riseley-Prichard
1955 Crystal Palace F1	30/07/1955	Jack Fairman
1955 Snetterton F1	13/08/1955	Peter Walker
1955 Oulton Park Gold Cup	24/09/1955	Peter Walker
1955 Castle Combe F1	01/10/1955	Peter Walker
1956 Goodwood F1	02/04/1956	Reg Parnell
1956 Aintree F1	21/04/1956	Reg Parnell
1956 International Trophy	05/05/1956	Reg Parnell
		Peter Walker
1957 Syracuse Grand Prix	07/04/1957	Jack Brabham
1957 Caen Grand Prix	28/07/1957	Tony Brooks
1957 International Trophy	14/09/1957	Noel Cunningham-Reid
1957 International Trophy	14/09/1957	Jack Fairman
1957 Moroccan Grand Prix	27/10/1957	Jack Brabham
1958 Goodwood F1	07/04/1958	Stirling Moss
		Tony Brooks
		Maurice Trintignant
1958 Aintree F1	19/04/1958	Stirling Moss
1958 International Trophy	03/05/1958	Tony Brooks
		Maurice Trintignant
1958 Caen Grand Prix	20/07/1958	Stirling Moss
1959 Goodwood F1	30/03/1959	Stirling Moss
		Maurice Trintignant

Non-championship races	Date	Driver
1959 Aintree F1	18/04/1959	Stirling Moss
1959 Oulton Park Gold Cup	26/09/1959	Stirling Moss
1960 Buenos Aires Grand Prix	14/02/1960	Maurice Trintignant
1960 Goodwood F1	18/04/1960	Stirling Moss
1960 International Trophy	14/05/1960	Stirling Moss
1960 Oulton Park Gold Cup	24/09/1960	Stirling Moss
1961 Goodwood F1	03/04/1961	Stirling Moss
1961 Brussels Grand Prix	09/04/1961	Stirling Moss
1961 Vienna Grand Prix	16/04/1961	Stirling Moss
1961 Aintree F1	22/04/1961	Stirling Moss
1961 Syracuse Grand Prix	25/04/1961	Stirling Moss
1961 Naples Grand Prix	14/05/1961	Giuseppe Maugeri
1961 Modena Grand Prix	03/09/1961	Stirling Moss
1961 Oulton Park Gold Cup	23/09/1961	Stirling Moss
1962 Brussels Grand Prix	01/04/1962	Stirling Moss
1962 Pau Grand Prix	23/04/1962	Maurice Trintignant
1962 International Trophy	12/05/1962	Maurice Trintignant
1962 Mallory Park F1	11/06/1962	Graham Hill
1962 Reims Grand Prix	01/07/1962	Maurice Trintignant
1962 Kanonloppet	12/08/1962	Graham Hill
1962 Oulton Park Gold Cup	01/09/1962	Jo Bonnier
1962 Mexican Grand Prix	04/11/1962	Ricardo Rodriguez
		Maurice Trintignant
1963 Pau Grand Prix	15/04/1963	Jo Bonnier
1963 Imola Grand Prix	21/04/1963	Jo Bonnier
1963 Syracuse Grand Prix	25/04/1963	Jo Bonnier
1963 International Trophy	11/05/1963	Jo Bonnier
1963 Solitude Grand Prix	28/07/1963	Jo Bonnier
1963 Kanonloppet	11/08/1963	Jo Bonnier
1963 Mediterranean Grand Prix	18/08/1963	Jo Bonnier
1963 Austrian Grand Prix	01/09/1963	Jo Bonnier
1963 Oulton Park Gold Cup	21/09/1963	Jo Bonnier
1964 Snetterton F1	14/03/1964	Jo Bonnier
1964 Goodwood F1	30/03/1964	Jo Bonnier
1964 Syracuse Grand Prix	12/04/1964	Jo Bonnier
1964 Aintree F1	18/04/1964	Jo Bonnier
1964 International Trophy	02/05/1964	Jo Bonnier
1964 Solitude Grand Prix	19/07/1964	Jo Bonnier
		Jo Siffert

Non-championship races	Date	Driver
1965 Race of Champions	13/03/1965	Jo Bonnier
		Jo Siffert
1965 Syracuse Grand Prix	04/04/1965	Jo Bonnier
		Jo Siffert
1965 Goodwood F1	19/04/1965	Jo Bonnier
1965 International Trophy	15/05/1965	Jo Bonnier
		Jo Bonnier
1965 Mediterranean Grand Prix	15/08/1965	Jo Siffert
		Jo Bonnier
1966 Syracuse Grand Prix	01/05/1966	Jo Siffert
1966 International Trophy	14/05/1966	Jo Siffert
1967 Race of Champions	12/03/1967	Jo Siffert
1967 International Trophy	29/04/1967	Jo Siffert
1967 Syracuse Grand Prix	21/05/1967	Jo Siffert
1968 Race of Champions	17/03/1968	Jo Siffert
1968 International Trophy	25/04/1968	Jo Siffert
1969 Race of Champions	16/03/1969	Jo Siffert
1969 International Trophy	30/03/1969	Jo Siffert
1970 Race of Champions	22/03/1970	Graham Hill
1970 International Trophy	26/04/1970	Graham Hill
1970 Oulton Park Gold Cup	22/08/1970	Graham Hill

Appendix 2

Bibliography

Information and photographs about the Rob Walker Team can be found in almost every history book on Grand Prix racing. Here is a selection of publications that give a more detailed picture of Rob Walker, his racing team and drivers.

Rob Walker	Michael Cooper-Evans
Private Entrant: Racing with Rob Walker	Michael Cooper-Evans
Alf Francis: Racing Mechanic	Peter Lewis
Tales from the Toolbox	Michael Oliver
Jo Siffert	Jacques Deschenaux
Stirling Moss - The Authorised Biography	Robert Edwards
Lotus 18	Ian Wagstaff

Selected museums

The Dorking Museum, 62 West Street, Dorking RH4 1BS
www.dorkingmuseum.org.uk

This wonderful collection of Rob Walker Racing Car models, which featured in the BBC's Bargain Hunt programme, can be seen on display at the Dorking Museum.

Brooklands Museum, Brooklands Road, Weybridge KT13 0SL
www.brooklandsmuseum.com

Donington Grand Prix Collection, Donington Lane, Castle Donington, Derbyshire DE74 2RP
www.donington-collections.co.uk

The Haynes International Motor Museum, Sparkford, Yeovil BA22 7LH
www.haynesmotormuseum.com

Rob Walker's beautiful 1936 Delahaye 135 Course at the The Haynes International Motor Museum.
(Courtesy of the Haynes International Motor Museum)

National Motor Museum, Beaulieu, Brockenhurst SO42 7ZN
wwwww.beaulieu.co.uk/attractions/national-motor-museum

Current Titles from The Cockerel Press

"A History of Brockham Park: from Gentleman's Residence to Award Winning Laboratory"
by Albert Bird

"A History of St Paul's School"
by Helen Wharmby

"Dorking's Famous Caves: History, Mystery and Geology"
by Richard Selley

"Early Medieval Dorking 600-1200 AD"
by Susannah Horne

"Mole Valley Open Gardens"
by David Drummond

"The Dorking Cockerel"

"The Museum Guide to Dorking: a Brief History of the Town and Surrounding Villages"
by Kathy Atherton

"The Tillingbourne Valley"
by George E Collins

"The Villages of Abinger Common and Wotton"
by Terry O'Kelly

"Time Gentlemen, Please: the Story of Dorking Pubs"
by David Langford and Jim Docking

"Suffragettes, Suffragists and Antis - the fight for the Vote in the Surrey Hills
by Kathy Atherton

**All available to buy at Dorking Museum,
62 West Street, Dorking, RH4 1BS**

THE
COCKEREL
PRESS